The FLUID MOTION FACTOR®

Understanding the Source of Exceptional Golf

Steven Yellin

Preface by David Leadbetter & Foreword by Buddy Biancalana

MASCOT® BOOKS

Nothing happens by accident in life. It may seem like circumstances sometimes come together and bring certain people into your life, but just as it is not by chance that the sun rises in the east and sets in the west, nothing happens in our life by chance. Though our lives might not reflect that precision on the surface, the deeper levels of intelligence unfolding our lives on a daily basis is the same intelligence that brings up the sun every morning.

There have been two people that have come into my life and have changed it. Permanently. And for the better. They brought that rare combination of wisdom and generosity and the ability to give of themselves unselfishly. Without their support, on many different levels, the knowledge represented in this book may never have been developed. They have supported me, encouraged me every step of the way, and as they know, there have been many, many steps. Chris Wege and Laura Yellin, my dearest of friends, this book is dedicated to the both of you. Humbly I thank you from the bottom of my heart and may your lives be blessed on every level.

-Steven Yellin

ISBN-13: 9781620867594
CPSIA Code: PRW0714A

Book design by Joshua Taggert

Printed in the United States

www.mascotbooks.com

The *FLUID MOTION FACTOR*®

Understanding the Source of Exceptional Golf

Steven Yellin

Preface by David Leadbetter & Foreword by Buddy Biancalana

Table of Contents

Preface

David Leadbetter

Having taught this great and frequently frustrating game of golf for about forty years to everybody from world number ones to total novices, this game is a mystery to even me, at times! Why is it when I look at a swing on the practice tee with my trained eye, and everything seems perfect, the ball is flying straight and true, the rhythm is languid, and when the player gets to the first tee, the ugly relation shows up? There is no consistency, no solid contact, shots go right and left, and frustration sets in. How can a player play a number of holes in a round of golf like a low-handicap player, and then inexplicably, play like a rank beginner?

How does a Tour player shoot 64 in the first round and 78 in the second? Why is it that swing keys that worked beautifully yesterday, then thinking the same swing keys today, don't work at all? This is all part of the fascination of the sport, and whether one calls good ball striking and scoring consistency, competence, or being in the zone, or whatever, it is extremely elusive.

As coaches, we are constantly trying to improve technique and mechanics to make the golf swing more repetitive and fundamentally sound. Yet, rarely do golfers reach their true potential in their games. They may taste success once in a while, but even at the highest level, the game is tough to figure out, especially when you bring in the putting component as well.

You do hear on occasions, "I am playing well" or "I have really got it." What is "it" when you have "it"? That, I suppose, is the Holy Grail and when a player has "it" for however long, they play their best golf.

You see this on the PGA tour when players have hot streaks and seem to play well for a number of tournaments in a row. When a player loses "it," they search and search, trying to recapture the magic. Certainly the problem could be a number of things: a swing mechanic flaw, an injury, some issue off the golf course, all affecting a player's confidence. However, I will also say that I have seen players who really appear to be swinging well, and yet the results are just not there.

In today's age of technology with high-speed video, 3D analysis, launch monitors, etc., we are able to detect the minutest flaws and suggest a fix—and in a short amount of time. Even with all this, the player frequently finds it difficult to put the club on the ball squarely and consistently. Somehow, there seems to be a block or disconnect in the system, interrupting the free flowing movement that is apparent when things are going well. A player could be doing their drills, working on the right stuff, and even thinking well and yet…

So I was most interested when I met Steven Yellin, a former Florida State High School singles tennis champion and All-Ivy player at the University of Pennsylvania and his associate, Buddy Biancalana, a former World Series championship winner with the Kansas City Royals. Through their experience in sports and Steven being involved in TM, Transcendental Meditation, for many years, Steven has developed a systematic and effective program to quiet the mind that allows athletes in all sports to consistently access what they already own. That is worth its weight in gold. It is a revolutionary approach that I had never been exposed to until Steven taught it to me. I use it now whenever I play. In the case of golf, you develop or recapture a powerful, free flowing swing, which even if one's mechanics are slightly off, one is able to miraculously self-correct at the point of contact and hit good shots. They call their approach the "Fluid Motion Factor"—FMF. It applies to all sports, and in fact, to any activity with movement or motion or that requires rhythm, i.e., dancing, piano, etc.

FMF is really not sports psychology in the true sense, which, I might add, I am a big fan of. Certainly, one needs to be in the right frame of mind, stick to a routine, be organized, and have a good attitude, etc.—areas that sports psychologists work hard on with players. FMF is, in my mind, the bridge between the psychology and the mechanical aspect of the game. In the case of golf, it is all about hitting good, solid, on-line shots with effortless power.

If you have worked hard on your game or are simply frustrated with your inconsistency and suffer from paralysis through analysis, FMF could help you immeasurably. I am a big advocate of technology to assist us to improve. We use it all the time at our academies, but FMF is a great counterbalance to this high-tech world we live in. The average golfer, who seems to have less time to play and practice than ever, is bombarded with more mechanical thoughts and complex theories than in any stage of golfing history. FMF allows you to simplify things, trust to a large extent what you already have and bring feel into the equation. After all, this is what the greats have done through the eras, from Tom Morris right up to Tiger Woods. This FMF approach is probably, and almost certainly, what you have experienced, whether you know it or not, when you have played your best golf!

I'm excited about the Fluid Motion Factor Program. I am always looking for new, cutting-edge approaches— although the concept behind this one is as old as the hills! We have included the program in our curriculum at our worldwide headquarters for the Leadbetter Golf Academies at ChampionsGate in Orlando, Florida. My goal is to do whatever necessary to help players of all abilities play their best golf. We utilize the technique aspect certainly. We have a sport psychologist, a physical trainer, a club fitter, and Callaway Performance Center, and now we offer the Fluid Motion Factor with Steven Yellin. This book will give you a taste of what FMF is all about. It will open your eyes to a new approach that may well be the tipping point of consistent golf for you—golf you know you are capable of playing, but somehow never achieve on a regular basis.

Enjoy the read and stay fluid!

Regards,
David Leadbetter
January 2014

Foreword

Buddy Biancalana

---///---

Having spent thirty-five years in and around professional baseball as a player, coach, agent and broadcaster, I have been exposed to many teaching techniques and philosophies. My interest in all these techniques stemmed from my Zone experience in the 1985 World Series in which I played the best baseball of my life. I played shortstop for the Kansas City Royals and almost won the MVP of the series. However, eighteen months later, I was out of the major leagues because I had no idea how to repeat that wonderful feeling of time slowing down, the mind becoming very quiet and the motion becoming effortless.

It was approximately seven years ago that Steven Yellin and I had our first of three consecutive lunches together. A mutual friend that knew we were both working in sports introduced us. Over those lunches, Steven shared a revolutionary understanding about sports and motion I had never heard before. Although I had never heard it before, I could sense profound wisdom and truth. Following our third lunch, Steven asked me to go to the driving range so he could show me how to elevate my golf game. In a matter of minutes, my game took a quantum leap. After about fifteen minutes of hitting balls, I told Steven that his knowledge would change how all sports are taught. I stand behind that comment today. It took about another minute on the range to agree to form our company, PMPM Sports-Zone Training and now the Fluid Motion Factor.

Over the last seven years of teaching our program to athletes in seven professional and fourteen amateur sports, I have been hesitant to make the statement to players, coaches and agents that this is going to change how sports are taught. After all, it is a very strong statement. But what you're about to read will revolutionize how athletes are taught and will enhance any teacher's ability to get the best out of their students. It comprehensively analyzes and explains that elusive X-Factor as to what fundamentally occurs when athletes in any sport play their best. As a teacher or as a player, I hope one day you have the opportunity to experience our program in whatever sport you play. It will help you reach your potential as an athlete and greatly increase your joy of the game.

Buddy Biancalana
Co-founder, PMPM Sports-Zone Training
zonetraining.net
fluidmotiongolf.com

Introduction

There is a revolution about to happen in golf.

There have been many revolutions in golf. The golf ball went through a revolution when it went from balata to surlyn to the current five-piece ball. The golf shaft went through a revolution when it went from wood to steel to graphite. Golf clubs went through a revolution when they became bigger and were manufactured with more forgiving materials. As a result of these changes, clubs became easier to hit and golf balls went farther.

Golf instruction went through a revolution when video analysis entered the picture in the 1990s. But the upcoming revolution will exceed the impact on the game more than all of the above—by a large margin. This revolution is the most fundamental revolution that can ever or will ever occur in the game. This revolution has to do with what has to happen in the mind in order to produce a fluid golf swing.

"Has to" is a very strong phrase as it leaves little room for debate. But this is the reality of the situation. Although there are many ways to successfully swing a golf club or to teach someone golf, there is only one way fluid motion can be produced in a golf swing. To produce fluid motion, the brain operates identically for all golfers. This is not from a sports psychology perspective but from a neurophysiological understanding of how motion is produced in the body. This means that when any golfer produces a fluid golf swing, whether they be a high, mid, low-handicapper, or a major tournament winner, they all experience identical processes in their mind.

Knowledge of how the mind produces a fluid golf swing is nothing new. Neuroscientists have understood it for the past fifty years. Why it has never been brought to the forefront of golf and, for that matter, every sport, is an excellent question. But now it has been brought to the forefront and it will revolutionize how golf is taught and played. It will challenge the status quo and it might shake up a few people along the way. But truth is truth and once the processes in the mind that produce fluid golf swings are understood by the custodians of the game, golf will change— for the better. The game will be easier to learn, easier to play, and will grow exponentially. It will be the most significant advancement in the history of the game. To be on the team that initiated this change is a great honor and great responsibility, and I feel very fortunate to be part of it.

The idea for this book came to me while teaching the

Fluid Motion Factor Program to the son of one of the greatest golf teachers in the history of the game, at the Concession Golf Club in Bradenton, Florida. The history of how a golf club got to be called The Concession Golf Club is a story in itself.

In the 1969 Ryder Cup, Jack Nicklaus conceded a very missable putt to Tony Jacklin on the 18th and final hole of the competition. This resulted in the first-ever tie between the United States and Great Britain. It was heralded as one of the noblest gestures of sportsmanship in golf. 37 years later Jack and Tony teamed together and designed and built a magnificent golf course in Bradenton that only extended the historic relationship between them. They aptly named their club The Concession Golf Club—certainly an odd, but apropos name.

As I was teaching this extremely gifted young player, who no doubt had the best instruction a golfer could have from an early age, he turned to me after a few minutes and bluntly proclaimed, "Practice to me is like homework—boring, very boring." I thought to myself that if he is saying this when he is eighteen-years old and he still has this feeling about practice, then his chances of succeeding as a professional golfer are probably not that good. Playing golf on the professional level demands continual practice.

I turned to him and asked if he wanted to make practice not only fun, but also more productive. I wasn't surprised when his face lit up and he answered, "Are you kidding? Of course!" I smiled inside, knowing what I was about to teach him would change his golfing career and exponentially accelerate his progress as a player. I then proceeded to instruct him in one of the most revolutionary programs ever introduced in sports—the Fluid Motion Factor Program.

Within a few minutes he was not only hitting the ball better, farther, and straighter, but a lightness came over his mind and body that turned him around 180 degrees. That was the beginning of a radical transformation in his practice sessions that would make practice something to look forward to, rather than something he wanted to avoid. I knew then and there I needed to write a book about his experience, which is probably repeated countless times, every day, all over the world with athletes in every sport and usually prevents very talented players from reaching their potential.

Golfers practice diligently and often very systematically but, in my opinion, and hopefully yours as well after you read this book, they need to understand something when they practice they are probably not even aware of. That something separates golfers on all levels. It is the elusive X-Factor—the hidden element that determines who wins a tournament or who doesn't even make the cut or who has a successful career as an athlete or who doesn't reach their potential. It is time to take that X-Factor, that "it" David Leadbetter talked about in the preface, and bring it out in the bright daylight and understand and analyze it from every angle.

So let the journey begin. Fasten your seatbelts, prepare to be taken on a fascinating adventure going deep into insights about golf and motion that lie far below the radar, and let's see where we end up at the end of our ride.

Chapter 1

In-N-Out

Here are two different stories from two different sports that paint the whole picture.

When Buddy Biancalana was six years old, he asked his mother, "Do I play for the Dodgers and then go to college, or do I go to college and then play for the Dodgers?" He was wrong on both counts; he neither played for the Dodgers nor went to college, but he was certainly thinking in the right direction.

In the 1978 Major League Baseball draft, Buddy was the number one pick for the Kansas City Royals. As a superstar shortstop at Redwood High School in Marin County, California, he was on the All-American team and caught the attention of John Schuerholz, the scouting director of the Royals. Schuerholz selected him in the first round and

Buddy was on his way to playing professional baseball.

Buddy moved up the ranks in the Royals' organization and eventually got his big break in September 1985, when the Royals were in the hunt for the American League divisional title. Manager Dick Howser replaced shortstop Onix Concepcion with Buddy and in a Pennant race that went right down to the wire, the Royals squeaked by the California Angels to win the American League Western Division. They then defeated the Toronto Blue Jays in the American League Championship Series and were headed to the World Series.

Something magical happened to Buddy in that series. Something happened to him that is the dream of every baseball player, in fact of every athlete, in every sport. He slipped deep into the Zone. And he picked the absolute best time in his career to do it—playing in the biggest games, in front of the biggest audience, with the biggest prize a baseball player can have.

But in his first at bat, he didn't get the job done. With a man on third, Howser called for a suicide squeeze. This is a bold and exciting play where the batter attempts to bunt while the runner at third base takes off for home on the pitch. John Tudor, the St. Louis Cardinal pitcher, threw a tailing fastball to Buddy in which he could not get his bat on and, subsequently, the runner was tagged out. While Buddy experienced disappointment and frustration as he walked back to the dugout, another feeling quietly and unexpectedly emerged. It was a feeling he was not accustomed to having after striking out.

He felt everything had slowed down—almost to the

point where he experienced the pitch moving in slow motion. And he felt very calm inside.

Buddy was an exceptional fielder, which was the reason Schuerholz drafted him in the first round. But he was known, in terms that are somewhat kind, as a light hitter. In the mid-80s, teams could accept a shortstop that was an exceptional defensive player, but not an outstanding hitter. Organizations at the time were not paying shortstops as much as they do today. Ozzie Smith, Buddy's counterpart in the series, heralded in a new world order at that position by being able to field and hit. So at the time, Buddy fit the mold at shortstop perfectly—a player who could make a game-saving play, but probably not get many game-winning hits.

Because he was not an exceptional hitter, he usually experienced time happening quickly at bat. Only the exceptional hitters experienced time moving slowly. Remember that famous Ted Williams quote: "The ball is moving so slowly, I feel I can see the seams." Buddy did not see those seams the majority of his career, but as he walked back to the dugout, seeing those seams became a distinct possibility.

He then went on a tear in the series.

At the time, he was playing on the only World Series team to lose the first two games at home and come back to win a series in seven games. He batted 73 points over his career average, made 31 errorless plays at shortstop, and was the second leading vote-getter for the MVP. Following the series he appeared on the David Letterman and Today shows. In other words, he had his solid fifteen minutes of fame. George Brett, the Hall of Fame third baseman, said that without Buddy's level of play, the Royals never would have won the series.

Eighteen months later Buddy was out of the major leagues.

He couldn't repeat how he played in that series and the harder he tried, the worse he played. Not only did he not understand how the Zone showed up at his doorstep in the World Series, but, just as importantly, he had no idea how to bring it back. He lived the dream once. He would not live it again.

This is the story of countless professional and amateur athletes in every sport. Somehow, someway, in big situations, they are able to access their full talent and ability and perform at the high level they are capable of. They live the dream and try to repeat that dream and often come up short. As you will read shortly, they usually look in the wrong place to repeat it.

Stewart Cink had a similar experience as Buddy is in the last round of the 2008 British Open. Cink played a dreamlike final round to get into a playoff with Tom Watson. He birdied four of the last eight holes and made a crucial twelve-foot putt on the 72nd hole. He then cruised to win his first and only major championship.

Afterwards, he made comments that underscore the essence of this book:

"You know you have those kinds of rounds when everything just slows down, and you feel you have complete control of the club and can control the distance and the shape of the shot. You never know when you are going to have those kinds of rounds or those kinds of feelings again, so you have to take

advantage of them whenever they show up."

Though Cink still plays on Tour, he has not been able to repeat the success he had in that British Open.

Both Buddy and Stewart are perfect examples of what this book is all about. They both went into the Zone, came out, and because they didn't know how they got there, realistically, how could they expect to practice something that would allow them to get there again? If an athlete does not fundamentally know what is happening when playing their best, how can they develop a practice routine that will allow them to repeat their best performances? The whole subject clearly needs significant clarification. In a very real way, they are just hoping and praying those feelings emerge when they compete again. Sometimes they do, but more often, they don't.

Let's dive into this problem right now and shed light on the most significant question in all of sports.

Chapter 2

The Ocean of Motion

It isn't rocket science—it's just common sense.

Golf is about motion, motion is about the muscles, and the operating system of the muscles is located in the mind. A logical and correct conclusion is that when someone is locked in and playing exceptionally well in any sport, something occurs in their mind that allows their muscles to produce fluid and effective motion. What that something is, is not exactly clear.

Though there is an intuitive sense that great athletes have minds that work more efficiently than not-so-great athletes, what that means is not exactly clear. It is as if they have a 12-cylinder Ferrari parked outside their house and every day they drive it to work. Some days, for whatever reason, they are able to use all 12 cylinders. This is when a superstar gets locked in and plays exceptionally well. Most of the time though, they only have access to 7 or 8 cylinders, and have to make do with that.

The unanswered question is even superstars are not too sure why they had access to all 12 cylinders on a particular day. Did Buddy and Stewart understand why they had access to all those cylinders? Probably not. The question is being asked not from a sports psychology perspective, but from a more fundamental neurophysiological perspective. No doubt confidence, self-belief, a strong desire to win, talent, excellent training habits, proper coaching, and other positive elements have to be present in order to perform at a high level. But the bottom line is that when the muscles are producing fluid and powerful motion on any given day, the operating system of the muscles has to be performing efficiently. How that happens and why that happens is the elusive X-Factor in every sport. Let's initially answer that question in terms of a concept we are all familiar with: muscle memory.

Muscle memory is not located in the muscles. It is located in the part of the brain known as the basal ganglia. This is how it works: when learning a motion, any motion, whether walking or swinging a golf club, the memory of those motions are deposited in the basal ganglia. Over a period of time, when enough motions have been deposited in the basal ganglia, a person grooves that motion, meaning it can be repeated on demand. It is similar to saving money in a savings account. Let's say you want to save $10,000. You go to the bank, fill out an application, and start depositing money in your account. You may put in $600 one month,

$300 another, $400 the following month, until you have saved your $10,000.

Now, regardless of when you go to the bank, your money is available. If you go next Tuesday, the money is there. If you go ten months from now, the money is there. If you go *ten years from now*, the money is there. *Whenever you go*, your funds are there.

The revolutionary understanding that can change how golf is taught and played is that muscle memory is no different. Practice deposits muscle memory in your brain. Once sufficient muscle memory has been accumulated, it will not disappear, just as the funds in your savings account will not disappear. As you will read later in the book, this is a career-changing understanding that can have enormous implications on a golfer's performance. Sufficient muscle memory can be defined as the ability to repeat a motion consistently, without pressure, on demand. The crucial question that forms the foundation of this book is, how can you consistently access what you already own? That is the question every athlete wants answered.

It is not as if Buddy and Stewart had to develop more muscle memory to play their best. They already had enough memory in the bank to play at a high level. In fact, enough muscle memory had been developed to play like that all the time. For whatever reason, they did not access what they already owned when they did not play well. When they slipped into the Zone, they simply accessed what was already theirs. When they went to the bank and wanted to withdraw a motion from their account, the teller just smiled and said, "You have access to all your funds today…take whatever you want, gentlemen!" And the muscle memory bank is a very special kind of bank—even when you withdraw funds, the principal is left untouched!

The ability to access muscle memory on demand is the slipperiest of slopes. It defines careers. One cannot be a bull in a china shop and demand the teller provide your funds whenever and wherever you want. You have to understand the very distinct and unchanging rules of the bank. The superstars in every sport have an intuitive feeling for the rules of the bank and honor and respect them, so when they do approach and ask the teller for a withdrawal, they usually get the response they want.

This separates athletes in every sport—not so much the difference in the amount of muscle memory they have in the bank (at any PGA tournament, you will see 140 players with just about equal funds!), but the ability to access what they own. Somehow, someway, the great ones, especially under pressure situations, usually get the response they want when they ask the teller for a withdrawal, and as a result, win major championships. But as you will see in this book, the rules of the bank lay well under the radar and are not well understood by the vast majority of golfers. One purpose of this book is to explain those rules.

****

Let's return to the operating system of the muscles.

Since golf is about motion, it is crucial to understand how motion, especially fluid motion, is produced in a golf swing from a neurophysiological perspective. Two parts of the brain that play a central role in producing motion are the pre-frontal cortex (PFC) and the motor system. The PFC, also called the CEO of the brain, oversees all processes in the mind. It is the discriminating intellect. The motor system is that part of the brain that communicates with the body to produce motion. When you first learn a motion, the PFC is very much engaged in the learning process. If a coach tells you to take the club back in a certain manner, the PFC oversees that process. But once enough muscle memory has been established, it becomes crucial for the PFC to stay out of the way.

In order to produce a motion, whether it is motion of walking across the street or motion of hitting a 300-yard drive, a signal is generated in the brain during the motion. Even if it feels like you are not thinking during a motion, there has to be a signal, an intention to generate a motion. Now here is the crucial point. Once a motion is grooved, which means enough money has been deposited in the bank, and a motion can be repeated on demand, if that signal is not intercepted by the PFC and goes directly to the motor system, the motion will be fluid and effective. I call this process the Fluid Motion Factor.

But, and it is a gigantic career-ending but, if a motion has been grooved and the signal is intercepted by the PFC during a motion and slightly delayed in moving to the motor system, the motion will not be fluid. That is because in the middle of a motion, the body is looking for direction from the motor system and basal ganglia and if that information is not seamlessly forthcoming, the circuitry controlling motion becomes clogged. Within the brain, there are too

Fluid Motion Factor

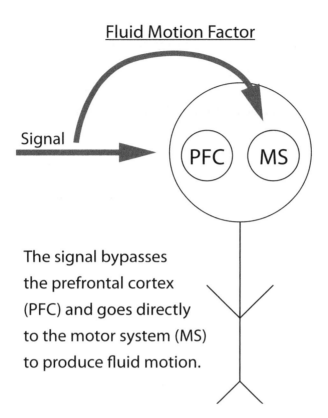

Signal

PFC   MS

The signal bypasses
the prefrontal cortex
(PFC) and goes directly
to the motor system (MS)
to produce fluid motion.

many processes occurring. As a result of the signal being intercepted and thinking becoming overactive, the bulkier muscles dominate the swing and nine times out of ten, the motion will not be successful.

There you have it—the most fundamental definition of what happens when a swing starts to go south and the first rule of the bank. It could be the pressure of the situation, fear of failure, fear of success. or any other combination of reasons why a motion starts to break down, but ultimately it comes down to the operating system of the muscles not performing correctly. If an engine is not tuned correctly, a car will not run smoothly. If a grooved swing breaks down, it is because the brain physiology is not operating correctly.

Signals being delayed even slightly in traveling to the motor system end careers.

If you took a video analysis of someone's swing in a tournament when they hit a bad shot, you would obviously see which parts of the swing broke down. But a question that has to be asked is, "Why on the previous shot did all the parts work correctly and on this shot, you came over the top, blocked it, snapped it, or did something that ended up with a poor result?" Ultimately, it is the brain physiology that controls the swing. When someone drops a ball after hitting a poor shot, they usually hit it pure. Why? It is not like all of a sudden they found their swing. It is because they used the brain physiology the way it is supposed to be used in order to swing well. A good swing can only occur when the brain physiology is operating correctly.

Let's dig down deeper in this operating system and see how some of the other parts work.

If you sat down with 100 great athletes and asked them how they felt when playing their best, their responses would most likely be divided into three categories:

1. Time slowed down.

The experience of time is controlled by neurons in the PFC and the motor system. When the PFC intercepts a signal, the neurons in the PFC will overshadow the neurons in the motor system and time will be experienced as moving quickly. Nobody shoots a 64, walks off the course, and says that time was moving quickly during the round. When Kobe Bryant scores 50 points in a game, he does not say that time moved quickly on the court that night.

What do they say? The opposite—time slowed down. Why? Because they have to. Athletes have to say this when playing their best because time experienced fast indicates the PFC intercepted the signal and delayed it in moving to the motor system. It is never beneficial when this happens because the Fluid Motion Factor automatically shuts down.

Ted Williams could supposedly see the seams on the ball at the plate because the neurons in his PFC did not overshadow the neurons in his motor system. Both Buddy and Stewart experienced time moving slowly when they had their Zone experiences. The same thing happens to any golfer when they have their best ball-striking day. Time has to be moving slowly when playing one's best, and this is one of the best indicators of accessing the Fluid Motion Factor. Just think of what you experienced when you played your best golf.

2. The mind became very quiet.

When Stewart shot his final round in the British Open, his mind was very quiet. When Buddy had his Zone experience in the World Series, his mind was very quiet. When you played your best, your mind became very quiet. The mind has to become quiet to play well and here is why.

The PFC is the discriminating intellect. When it intercepts the signal in the middle of a motion, it will always feel like the mind is engaged. This is rarely beneficial because the signal will then be delayed in moving to the motor system and, as a result, the bulkier muscles will dominate, especially those in the upper arms. It will then feel like you are muscling the ball. No one shoots a 64, walks off the course and says, "*My intellect was really engaged today. I was thinking on every shot.*" What they usually say is the opposite—they weren't thinking at all.

Tiger tells a fascinating story on his DVD called Tracking the Tiger that exemplifies this point. If you were unaware of the dynamics of how fluid motion is produced in the body, you might think it was a story from the *Twilight Zone*. He says, "*There have been key shots in major tournaments where I took the club out of the bag and I didn't remember anything until I saw the ball land on the green.*"

Meanwhile, commentators Johnny Miller or Nick Faldo are in the booth saying, "*Look at Tiger's focus, look at his determination and concentration,*" while Tiger's actual experience is 180 degrees from that! "*I took the club out of the bag and didn't remember anything until the shot was finished.*"

He made that statement because one has to make those kinds of statements when they are playing their best. If the intellect is engaged during a motion, the body will not be free. The bulkier muscles will dominate during the motion and you will probably come over the top, won't release at impact, have poor tempo, or a host of other problems that you never want to have. The pre-frontal cortex has to go "offline" to play well. The mind has to shut down. This is the origin of popular sayings like 'playing out of one's mind' or 'going mindless' when playing. For most of Tiger's career, that was the space he lived in. It is the reason why he was able to swing with freedom in pressure situations.

One year in Orlando I was working with a former two-time U.S. Open winner. After a few holes he turned to me and unexpectedly said that one of his main goals for the rest of his career was to be able to "swing with abandonment" like Tiger. Tiger's fellow pros knew how much freedom Tiger had with his swing at the height of his domination, and they also knew this was one of the main reasons he won so often.

3. The motion was fluid and effortless.

The motor system is comprised of three parts, but the real genius of those parts is the cerebellum. The cerebellum is responsible for managing three critical things during a motion:

1. Firing the fast-twitch muscles at the appropriate time.

2. Tracking where the body is and where the body has to be in split second increments in order to execute a fluid motion.

3. Allowing the parts of the swing to fire in sequence, which smooths out the motion.

The fast-twitch muscles are the muscles responsible for generating faster clubhead speed with less effort. When they fire at the right time and with the right amount of action, balls explode off drivers and irons are hit crisper. They of course have to fire in sequence with the rest of the swing. If they don't fire, the bulkier, core muscles will dominate the swing and that is the cause of not releasing at impact and muscling and guiding the ball.

There is a correct sequence in a finely tuned swing. One can say this sequence represents an energy flow from the lower body to the upper body to the arms, then hands and finally to the club. In an inefficient swing, energy gets blocked somewhere along the way. Maybe it stops in the upper body or the arms and when this occurs, power is lost. The cerebellum ensures that energy flows smoothly from one part of the swing to the next. A swing can be said to be "fluidized" when this occurs.

The cerebellum also tracks where the body is and where it has to be in order to produce an effective motion. This tracking is occurring in milliseconds. This means if the cerebellum is operating efficiently and any split-second corrections are needed in the swing, the body will be liquid enough to make those corrections and bring the club back to square at impact and hit an acceptable shot. In other words, if at the top of your swing you realize you are in trouble because you have the club in the wrong position and if you make your normal move on the ball you will most likely block it, the cerebellum will make the body liquid enough to redirect the club on the way down and square it up at impact. This could transform a potentially disastrous outcome into an acceptable shot.

Better than the best driver, the best putter, the best clubs, the best swing key, or even the best coach, if the cerebellum is firing on all cylinders that day, you are going to be a satisfied golfer at the end of the round. When the origin of motion, the brain physiology, is operating correctly, you will always give yourself the best chance of playing well. When it is not, your chances decrease significantly.

When players make key shots under pressure, the cerebellum will always be the silent star of the show as it allowed the body and the swing to experience freedom, the parts to fire in sequence and the motion to be smooth. When players don't perform well under pressure, though it may be obvious what broke down when TV commentators analyze the swing, the origin of the problems can usually be traced back to the cerebellum not functioning correctly.

Using the above understanding of how the brain functions when playing one's best, the Zone can easily be described in terms of distinct neurophysiological functions. It should not be understood as some mysterious state that comes and goes on its own volition. It is the state that all athletes aspire to be in and the more knowledge one has of it, the better chance one has to be in it. Certainly the swing was working well when someone has an excellent ball-striking round, but the fundamental question that should always be asked is, "*Why was the swing working so well that day?*" Without being able to answer that question, one will never thoroughly understand why they play exceptional golf. The dynamics of the Fluid Motion Factor provide that explanation. It demystifies an area not well understood and offers a clear picture as to what occurs when someone plays their best.

Chapter 3
Paradigm Shifting

A paradigm is the way we understand a situation. For instance, we all have our own paradigm of understanding life. Some of us feel we are in control of our destiny, some feel we are victims of random circumstances, and some of us don't have any particular way we understand life at all, which is also a paradigm. Paradigms give direction and stability in life. They are crucial for growth and advancement.

The same is true in golf. Within the context of the ideas written in this book, there will be a few significant paradigm shifts needed before you can give yourself a better chance of reaching your full potential as a golfer. The first has to do with understanding motion from the most fundamental level. That is a significant and below-the-radar paradigm shift. It is a shift that most likely will go against how you have been taught in any sport you have played. But ultimately, it is absolutely necessary if you want to understand a golf swing from the most fundamental level. Here is the magical sentence:

Once a swing has been grooved, it needs to be understood as a by-product of the processes in the mind that produce it.

This is the big 180-degree shift. This is the paradigm on which you should base your practices and the future development of your game. It should be the foundation in which you grow as a golfer.

Most likely, your understanding of a golf swing and how to successfully reproduce a golf swing is to reproduce the motion. That is the paradigm in which you probably have lived your entire golf career. On one level, it is an absolutely correct paradigm. The club has to be taken back at a certain angle, set at the top at a certain angle, and has to start downward at a certain angle. If all of these things don't happen correctly, you probably won't hit a solid shot. But there is one fundamental principle that has to be kept in mind in order to understand the whole picture. If you are an accomplished player, you have already deposited enough swings in your account to have a grooved motion. That means all that is needed to play consistent golf is to access what you already own. In order to do that, the operating system of the muscles has to be functioning correctly. So, executing the parts of the swing correctly depends on the operating system working efficiently. Ultimately, and in the final analysis, a correct motion is not so much dependent on the parts of the swing working correctly, but on the mind operating correctly so the parts of the swing can operate correctly.

This is the most fundamental paradigm shift one can make. Since golf is about motion and motion is about the muscles, in order to repeat a good motion, the source of that motion has to be operating efficiently. If the Fluid Motion Factor shuts down during a swing, the parts of the motion will most likely shut down no matter how much practice you have put in or how many excellent shots you have previously hit.

In my opinion, the major mistake golfers make in practice and in competition is they think they have to open a new savings account every time they play—meaning they feel they need to go to the bank, fill out the necessary papers and start from scratch to save up another $10,000. This is the paradigm in which they operate. That is just not the case. Remember, once the $10,000 is there, it will always be there. Look what happens on tour every week. There are 140 beautiful golf swings out there, so beautiful swings are not the distinguishing characteristic of who wins that week. The key element is that for whatever reason—the stars lining up, biorhythms, waking up with a deep belief in oneself for those four days, finding a new girlfriend, reading an inspiring book—it could be a host of things, but when the player that won that week, when they went to the teller on the majority of their shots, the teller responded with the beautiful career changing response, *"Take whatever you want."*

It is crucial to understand why exceptional swings or rounds occur and why the right responses are given when you see that teller. Stewart's swing was obviously mechanically sound during the final round of the British Open, and Buddy's mechanics at bat and in the field during the World Series were close to picture-book perfect. They did things during those events they had done thousands of times correctly—only they picked the right time and under intense pressure to do them.

But more fundamental than their motion being sound and consistent is that the origin of their motion was fine-tuned during those events. For whatever reason, the operating system of the muscles was working as well as it could and as a by-product and only as a by-product, the body performed at its highest level. It's not as if they woke up and all of a sudden found they had $15,000, rather than $10,000, in their account. They just had access to all of that $10,000 and that was all that was needed to get the job done.

Every golfer wants to repeat their best performance as often as they can. If they have $10,000 in the bank, they always want to access the majority of that $10,000. If they have $8,000, they want a positive response when they ask the teller for that amount. But if one is not crystal clear as to why they received the responses from the teller that day that allowed them to play so well, is it realistic to think they will get positive response the majority of the times they tee it up? Probably not. In many ways, they are just rolling the dice and hoping for the best.

As Cink said in his quote, he was not too sure why those magical rounds appear at his doorstep, and Buddy had the same response. When you played your best, can you explain why you did so on that day and not on another? That is the most fundamental question you can ask yourself and most golfers cannot thoroughly answer it.

But the answer is simple and always the same—on your best days you accessed the Fluid Motion Factor. The operating system was firing on all cylinders. The brain physiology was used the way it was meant to be used in order for the body to perform at its highest level. If both of these very gifted athletes had a clear and comprehensive understanding of why they played so well in those situations (and had a systematic program that allowed them to access the Fluid Motion Factor more consistently), they most likely would reach their full potential as athletes. But because they did not understand motion from the most fundamental perspective and they did not have the correct paradigm when they practiced, their practice was not associated with a thorough understanding of how fluid motion is produced. They became too preoccupied with the by-product of accessing the Fluid Motion Factor, the actual motion, and not a thorough understanding of why that motion was produced.

This is similar to having a tree outside your window with beautiful fruits, flowers, leaves, and branches. The roots of the tree are underground and out of sight and, unless you have a thorough understanding of those roots, you will not have a thorough understanding of why the tree looks so beautiful. Without a thorough understanding of how to nourish the source of the intelligence of the tree, you will never understand why the fruits and flowers of the tree grow so beautifully. The same is true about motion.

A thorough understanding of the source of motion is

necessary before you can fully understand why you played well one day and not well the next. Once you have that understanding, the next shift in your thinking should be when you play well, certainly congratulate the parts of the swing that worked well that day, but first and foremost congratulate the operating system that allowed those parts to work so well. Understand the tree from the roots and understand the swing from the source of the swing. When you start living in that paradigm, magical things can happen.

****

The second major paradigm shift has to do with what I call mixing the perfect cocktail. Just as a perfect cocktail has the right amount of ingredients (and stirred, not shaken!), a perfectly-executed golf swing has the right amount of focus, concentration, and determination. The problem is that most golfers think that more concentration, focus, and determination result in better shots. This leads to the incorrect conclusion that on any given shot, in any given tournament, the player who has most the concentration and focus has the best chance of winning.

This is just not true.

Granted, concentration, focus, and determination are absolutely necessary to play well, but the only element that equates to execution is accessing the Fluid Motion Factor. Just think how you felt when you played your best. Were you focused? Of course you were. Were you concentrating? Yes. Were you determined? No doubt you were. But think how balanced those attributes were. And think about the lightness you felt during the round.

Would you characterize your best ball-striking days as something that resulted from intense focus, determination, and concentration? Probably not. You would most likely characterize those career rounds or excellent ball-striking days as something that felt simple and effortless. You probably walked off the course scratching your head and thinking, *That felt so simple. How the heck did I do that and why can't I do it all the time?*

In those career rounds you mixed the perfect cocktail. Focus, determination, and concentration were there, but they were balanced. And by being balanced, you had enough of those qualities present, in just the right amount, to execute excellent shots. And that amount was far less then you thought you needed to play excellent golf. It may be somewhat confusing because it always feels so simple to play great golf, yet you most likely have always felt that you have to be very focused to play well. But in reality, you probably need about 50% less focus, concentration, and determination than you think you need.

50%!

That is a lot. But that is about all the operating system needs to perform efficiently and sometimes even less. The brain physiology works efficiently under certain circumstances. It is very much like a car engine that needs to be tuned in a certain way to run well. If it is not tuned correctly, for instance, if the air-to-fuel ratio is off just slightly, the car will not run efficiently. And in golf, if there is an overabundance of focus or concentration, the swing will eventually break down. The swing breaks down when the Fluid Motion Factor breaks down. We all know what happens when the mixture is not right when we play. Here are two classic examples.

David Leadbetter was an accomplished golfer in his younger days and had aspirations to play professional golf. In the European Tour Q-School one year, in the middle of his fourth and final round, he knew he was more or less out of contention and thought to himself, *Ah, the heck with it,* and essentially gave up the idea he was going to get his playing card.

He then proceeded to blister the course. He eagled the Par 4 12th hole and the only thing standing between him getting his Tour card at the end of the round was a ten-foot putt on the 18th hole. That putt barely lipped out and David's career path was forever changed. Instead of South Africa getting another talented professional to play on the European Tour, the world got an extraordinarily gifted teacher who has had a huge impact in the game. In hindsight, I am not too sure David regretted that lip-out and I know Nick Faldo, Nick Price, Ernie Ells, and thousands of other golfers didn't as well!

The second story is about Willy Pumerol, a young professional player from the Dominican Republic. Willy was going through the first stage of Q-School for the PGA Tour in 2012. He shot 72, 70, and 71 in the first three rounds and after the third round, he felt he didn't really have a chance to advance to the next stage.

He then shot a 65.

In both stories, the point is obvious. Here two excellent golfers involved in important tournaments and in the beginning stages of the tournaments, both were over-concentrating and over-focused, i.e., the fuel-to-air ratio was off and they mixed the wrong cocktail. They then shot themselves out of contention. Then almost subconsciously, they found the right amount of concentration and focus in order to get the response they were looking for when they approached the teller. These two stories are repeated thousands (make that hundreds of thousands) of times every year in golf.

Before David and Willy teed it up on the first day, both were at a disadvantage. Because of the importance of the tournament they equated low rounds with increased focus and determination. They had the wrong paradigm as to what it would take to play well. As a result, they violated the rules of the bank and were disappointed in the response they got when they approached the teller and asked for a withdrawal. Then suddenly, somehow, they quickly understood the subtle rules of that institution and were resurrected, but in both cases, too late.

In order to play your best, the right combination of focus and determination needs to be present. Just think about the best you have ever played. In reflection, focus, concentration and determination were there, but they were balanced. And they were probably experienced as "softer"—meaning they didn't dominate your awareness. When thoughts don't dominate your awareness, you will not be mentally and physically drained after the round. The overabundance of focus and concentration systematically shuts down the Fluid Motion Factor. The constant shutting down of the Fluid Motion Factor is exhausting to the mind and the body and prevents them from operating efficiently and playing consistent golf.

But because golfers do not have the correct paradigm or understanding about this, they place themselves at a distinct disadvantage even before they hit their first shot. From a neurophysiological perspective, a golfer has to enjoy their round in order to play well. This point was emphasized to me by Dr. Fred Travis, a well-respected neurophysiologist and director of the Center for Brain, Consciousness and Cognition at Maharishi University of Management in Iowa, a university where all the faculty, staff, and students practice the Transcendental Meditation Program. Extensive conversations over many years with Dr. Travis about how the brain functions allowed me to fine-tune the Fluid Motion Factor program.

Some years ago Dr. Travis was hired by the Norwegian Olympic Athletic Committee to determine why some national team members regularly placed high in national and international competitions and why other team members, who are as gifted and have similar training habits, do not. Dr. Travis determined that the brains of athletes who regularly placed high were operating more efficiently than the brains of those who did not. Their brains were operating more holistically and coherently. This research is discussed in our first book, *The 7 Secrets of World Class Athletes*.

Dr. Travis made it crystal clear to me that when an athlete's brain operates more efficiently, they will always enjoy the experience—in fact, they don't have a choice. A more coherent operating brain has to be associated with feelings of joy and happiness in competition. It is very difficult to play exceptional golf and not be happy, free and comfortable inside. Over-concentration and over-focus shut those feelings down in a nanosecond.

Just ask Rory McIlroy or Darren Clark. In 2011, Rory had quite a learning experience about this in the Masters and the U.S. Open tournaments. And Darren, because of his experience over a long career as a professional, had success when it counted most.

In the final round of the 2011 Masters, McIlroy had a comfortable four-shot lead after shooting 65, 69, and 70. It looked like this potential superstar was finally going to break through and be the next number one golfer in the world. But he shot 80 in the final round and finished tied for fifteenth.

What did he say about that 80? In his own, very candid words:

"I came out and was trying to be this player that I'm not. I was trying to be ultra-focused, tunnel-visioned, which just isn't like me. I'm usually pretty chatty and sort of looking around and being quite relaxed about the whole thing."

And those feelings were evident based on his expression and body language in that final round—they were anything but light. It looked as if he was walking around with a heavy load on his mind and his performance reflected that. He was over-focused and over-determined and a final round 80 emphasized that fact.

Fast-forward to the U.S. Open at Congressional two months later. Again Rory has a comfortable lead going into the final round. Everyone was wondering if he was going to hold it together or have another Augusta meltdown.

Well, he did hold it together and shot a smooth 68 to win by a spectacular eight shots. And his body language was markedly different than at Augusta. He looked comfortable and relaxed, almost as if he was playing a practice round, which was noticeably different from the last time he held the lead going into a final round at a major.

Darren Clark had a similar positive experience going into the final round of the 2011 British Open. With a slim one-shot lead over Dustin Johnson, many thought Clark, who had never won a major, would not be able to get the job done on Sunday.

He got the job done. He shot a 70 to win the tournament he most desired to win by three shots over Phil Mickelson. During that round, he was laughing and smiling and, just like Rory in the final round of the U.S. Open, he looked as if he was having a grand old time. Afterwards, his words resemble what Rory felt in the final round of the U.S. Open:

"I'm a bit of a normal bloke, aren't I? I like to go to the pub and have a pint, fly home, buy everybody a drink, just normal. There are not many airs and graces about me, and I was a little bit more difficult to deal with in my earlier years, but I mellowed some. Just a little bit. But I'm just a normal guy playing golf, having a bit of fun."

The point is abundantly clear. Obviously, focus, concentration, and determination are needed in order to play exceptional golf, but not as much as you think. And changing your paradigm as to what produces excellent golf shots and winning tournament scores is highly recommended. You should understand motion as a by-product of accessing the Fluid Motion Factor and when you do this, you will have a distinct advantage over the field and have a much better chance of reaching your full potential as a golfer.

****

Imagine a mythical tournament where you hit a ball to a target in front of you and if you didn't like the results, you can turn around 180 degrees and hit the ball anywhere you want. Then you could choose which shot you wanted to play. Since the second shot had no target, that is, wherever it ended up was perfect, you would always choose the second shot. In this dream-like mythical Land of Oz tournament, do you think you would ever make a bad swing on the second shot? 90% of the time (maybe even more), probably not.

That thought leads us to the next paradigm shift—a paradigm shift that is counter-intuitive, but nevertheless true:

A good swing cannot break down. What breaks down when you do not swing well is your ability to access what you already own.

Now let's take that mythical tournament mentioned above and make it even more mythical. If you don't like the shot you hit on the first try hitting a target, you can hit as many shots as you like at the same target until you do like one.

How many shots do you think you would you hit before you hit one that is acceptable? Three, eight, twenty-six? The point is that it doesn't matter. Eventually you would hit one that is acceptable. And that is exactly the point. Eventually you would hit one that is acceptable because you did not violate the rules of the bank and that allowed you to access what you already own.

Returning to this mythical tournament, let's set up a competition between whoever is the current number one player in the world and any other PGA touring professional. The number one player on Tour only gets one shot. The other player gets as many shots as he wants. Who do you think would win every time they teed it up? Then let's set up a normal competition where both just get one shot. Who do you think would win that competition the majority of the time?

In the first competition, eventually the PGA player that is not number one would be able to access what he owns. Chances are the number one player in the world would not be able to consistently do that with just one shot. But in a real-world competition, the number one player in the world has the ability to access the majority of his funds utilizing one swing, (that is why he is the number one player in the world) whereas the other pro can't do that as consistently. That one fact separates the two.

Every time you practice, swings are deposited into your muscle memory bank. Your muscle memory does not leave you. Once the swing is in the bank, it will always be in the bank. What separates players on every level is the ability to consistently access it. The rules of the bank are the same for everyone. Those that break through don't violate those rules as often as those that stay in the middle of the pack. The PFC, cerebellum, basal ganglia, motor system dynamics work identically for every player. Can you really say that any player has a far superior swing than everyone else? Certainly the top players have great swings, but they are not in a different league. The top players are the top players because they have the ability to more consistently access what they already own. They simply don't violate the rules of the bank as often as lower-ranked players. They have somehow figured out what those rules are and they honor and respect them every time they tee it up.

Here are three stories I heard over the past twelve months that leads us to the last paradigm shift.

The first story is from a very gifted golfer who won the junior world championship and has played in a number of major championships, including the U.S. Open and the British Open, but has not really reached his potential as a player. Last year he worked with a coach who felt he was not committed enough to his practice swing in his pre-shot routine. His coach asked, "*If you are not committed enough to your practice swing, how can you be committed to your real swing when you hit the ball?*" So all they did for one year was practice being more committed to the practice swing.

This player almost quit the game.

The second story came from another player who said he worked on having the exact pre-shot routine on every shot— down to almost timing it to the exact second.

This player has gone sideways the whole year.

The third story comes from a well-known coach that said it is crucial to not only pick out a target when you hit a shot, but to pick out a precise part in that target. For instance if you pick a tree you want to hit over, pick out a leaf on that tree as your target.

All three strategies reflect a common sentiment in golf

that the more concrete your goals are on any given shot, the better chance you have of executing it. Actually, the opposite is true, which leads us to our last paradigm shift:

The more abstract your goals are when you play, the better chance you have of accessing the Fluid Motion Factor.

Golfers are always trying to repeat their best days. Characteristics of those days often include not even remembering what score they had when they finished the round. Other characteristics include not remembering much about the round as a whole, similar to Tiger saying that often in key shots in major tournaments, he took the club out of the bag and didn't remember anything until he saw the ball land on the green. Golfers talk in terms of abstractions when they play their best, not concrete expressions. They don't say, "Well I played great today because I had the same routine on every shot," or "I zeroed in on an exact target on every shot." They don't say, "Well I finally got my wrist in the right position at the top of the swing and this allowed me to attack the ball from the inside." They usually talk in terms of feelings or having that elusive "it" that David Leadbetter talks about in the preface.

The reason they talk in terms of abstractions rather than in concrete terms, about their best rounds is because when the mind gets very quiet, it starts operating in what I call a field of abstraction. A good way of understanding this is a comparison between classical art and my favorite kind of art: cubism. A classical artist such as Rembrandt paints exactly what he sees. This contrasts with how the cubists, such as Picasso or Braque, paint. They break down reality into "cubes" that give a version of what they are seeing, but certainly do not reflect exactly what their eyes saw when they looked at the object they were painting. Interestingly enough, physics went through a radical transformation at about the same time as art, understanding reality not in terms of atoms, but in terms of more abstract levels of reality, where light, for instance, can be understood as a wave and as a particle. Modern music emerged around the same time.

This deeper understanding of the arts and science could reflect the deeper levels the mind experiences when playing exceptional golf. When playing well, the mind almost feels like it is going into a transcendental state and is losing the concrete boundaries that usually keep it in prison when not playing well. The mind feels restricted when goals and boundaries are very concrete. It restricts the ability to access the Fluid Motion Factor. Just remember the freedom you had when you played well. Do you think freedom emerged when you gave yourself restrictive goals such as having the exact same amount of time on each shot or picking out a leaf on a tree or hinging the wrists perfectly at the top of the swing?

I don't think so.

When the mind starts to move towards the field of abstraction, and not so caught up in doing something exactly correct, but having almost a vague idea of what to do, such as getting the ball in the general vicinity of a target rather than in a precise spot, it tends to free the mind and allow for greater freedom in a shot. If this is the kind of thinking you have when you have your best rounds, shouldn't it be the kind of thinking you have all the time?

Chapter 4

Enough Is Enough

My favorite golf story is about Jack Nicklaus. Jack won eighteen majors, but in my opinion, he did something more impressive in his career than winning all those majors. It is something that goes to the core of this book and serves as a lesson to golfers everywhere. In major championships he was second nineteen times, in the top three forty-eight times, in the top five fifty-six times, and seventy-two times he was in the top ten.

Talk about consistency! In my mind, those stats are more impressive than the eighteen times he won. To be so consistent in majors year in and year out is off the charts impressive and actually quite mind-boggling.

Jack was a fader of the ball. Like Lee Trevino said, "You can talk to a fade, but a hook won't listen." Tiger feels the same way, because that is also the natural shape of his shot. Jack, like all of us, would go to the range before a round and hit balls. But what he did on the range before a tournament, especially before major championships, was one of the key ingredients to his success.

He would see if he was fading or drawing the ball that day. Then he would take that shot and play it the whole round. This approach is quite radical versus today's understanding of the game. In today's game, you are either a fader or a drawer of the ball and that is what you take into the round…every round. You would be hard-pressed to find anyone that has the strategy Jack had. But Jack knew he had a secret weapon. He knew that just about every time he teed it up, his cerebellum would be working correctly. You can shoot a 65 with either a fade or a draw, but it would be difficult to shoot a 65 without the cerebellum working properly. The result of having that secret weapon? Well you read about the results above—the most spectacularly consistent record in major championships in the history of golf.

Jack had a deep insight into how his swing works, probably without fully understanding how the brain physiology operates. For sure he knew the feeling of that space when the Fluid Motion Factor was accessed and how to access it, and in the final analysis, as long as you arrive in that space when playing, that is all that is needed. His consistency was due to his ability to consistently access the genius of the cerebellum, the part of the motor system responsible for ensuring the correct energy flow in a swing and for timing. The cerebellum also tracks the body during a motion—where it is and where it has to be in milliseconds in order to execute a fluid motion. It allows the body to make last second corrections in a swing so an acceptable shot can be hit even if some mechanical flaws occur.

Better than good tempo, better than the correct way of setting the club at the top, better than finding the slot on the way down, if you really needed to pick one aspect of your swing to be working on any given day in any given tournament, you would be very wise to choose the cerebellum working properly. Why? Because if the cerebellum is working properly that day, you will have excellent timing. It will give you the ability to make last minute adjustments, enabling the club to come back to square at impact and hit solid shots with less than solid swings.

In my opinion, this was the secret weapon that Nicklaus brought to tournaments. He knew he couldn't repeat the same swing with the same ball flight every time he teed it up. No one can. He also knew there would be slight variations in his swing on any given day and that no one is an Iron Byron, a mechanical machine that can reproduce thousands of identical swings. So when he went to the range and saw the swing that was dealt him that day, he accepted it and changed his game plan accordingly. No doubt he hit the ball a mile, had masterful course management and deft putting, but if his cerebellum had not been firing on all cylinders when he teed it up, he would never have the record he did.

The moral of the story is simple. If you have enough money in the bank, your priority should be to work on the ability to access what you already own. Another way of putting this is in the form of a question: **When are you going to stop working on your swing and start being able to consistently access what you already own?** Another way to ask this question is: *If you were able to take the swing you use on the range and play with that swing in tournaments, would you be satisfied?*

The vast majority of professionals on all the Tours and probably most golfers would answer "yes." But because they are not doing what Nicklaus did his whole career and because they do not have a thorough understanding of motion and how to repeat motion from the most fundamental level, they are living too often in the mythical land of the capital "T".

The land of Tinkering.

Golfers are constantly trying to do this and do that to perfect their swing because they think if they are only able to get the club in this position or that position, somehow that will take them to the winner's circle and make their career as a golfer. In the developmental stages of a golfer, or when a golfer is going through an important swing change, that is an absolute necessity because poor mechanics rarely lead to good results.

In the beginning stages of learning golf, it would be wise to correctly learn the swing from a qualified PGA or LPGA professional. But, most golfers, at a certain stage in their development, have solid enough mechanics to play well. If they are consistent on the range, most likely their swing is grooved enough that they don't have to be constantly working on it. Then it is time to more or less shut the book on the mechanics of the swing and work on accessing what is already owned.

Here are a few stories to highlight that point.

Shelly Liddick, the 2012 and 2013 LPGA National Coach of the Year had a successful college career playing on the University of Alabama, Birmingham golf team. But she was always living in the 'T' land, working on this or that in her swing. One day PGA professional Chuck Hogan (her future husband!) came up to her and asked her a question that threw her for a loop: "Shelly, when will you finally be done with your swing?" When she realized the answer to that question was "Never," it woke her up instantly and she stopped tinkering with it. From that point on, she played more consistently and enjoyed it more.

Rick Fehr, a former professional player on the PGA tour, told the second story to me.

When Rick graduated from college he was the number two golfer in the country behind Lanny Wadkins. Rick was a superstar golfer in college, winning multiple tournaments every year and picked as a sure bet to be a star on the PGA Tour. In Rick's career, as he likes to say, he was 2 for 400, meaning that in the 400 tournaments he played, he won twice. He explained in hindsight that when he graduated college, if he did not change one thing in his swing, he felt he would have won fifteen times on Tour and been in the hunt in multiple majors. But because he felt he had to up the ante when he graduated college and take his swing to another level in order to compete on the PGA Tour, he worked on it for the next twenty years. In reality, he had a good enough swing to win multiple times the moment he teed it up in his first professional tournament. A good enough swing was always there; it was the correct paradigm that was missing.

The third story comes from someone that had great early success on the PGA Tour. He won two major championships and a Players Championships. This all happened early in his career. He thought he was going to win four or five times a year on Tour and win many more majors. This player was a flipper of the club, meaning he sometimes got it stuck on the way down and had to flip it at the last minute to hit a good shot. Well, he was quite a flipper—a two-time major winner, Players Champion, eight-time winner on Tour kind-of-flipper. Then, a well-known teaching professional got in his head and told him that if he just fixed his swing and stopped flipping, he could be even better and win more often. He bit the bullet and went to work on changing his swing.

He never really played consistently again. He didn't win any more tournaments after he won a major in the late 1990's. Later he told a good friend of mine that with hindsight, even though he could do three or four mechanical things wrong in his swing, including flipping the club, if he had one element working, he could get away with it and still play very, very well. When he started to do surgery on his swing, that element was lost and he couldn't regain it. What was that one element? Timing. And we return back to the cerebellum—the origin of timing in a golf swing and the best friend you can have when you play.

Now, let's return to the question as to when golfers should stop working on their swing. According to Shelly, someone very qualified to offer a response, this should happen when two things occur:

1. When they have an understanding of the parts and the wholeness of a swing.

2. When they are consistent on the range and most of the time on the course.

Those parameters would probably apply to a majority of golfers. Most golfers have gone through the developmental stages, played enough rounds, hit enough good shots, so that it may be time to stop working on their swing, or at least minimize going into the tweaking mode and start working on their ability to access what they already own.

The concept that a golfer has to do things exactly the same way every time they swing may shut down the Fluid Motion Factor. Golfers may have three or four different swings that work on any given day. This is what Nicklaus had. Former PGA Tour winner David Ogrin told me a story that also reflects this sentiment. Playing in the PGA Tour opening tournament in Hawaii one year, on a routine 7-iron, he realized during his back swing that the club was in a different position than normal. He obviously had to continue the swing and ended up sticking it two feet. He had an epiphany then and there that he probably had more than one swing that could get the job done.

As long as the body is malleable enough, you can be effective with variations of your normal swing. The key is to access the Fluid Motion Factor so the body can make the necessary adjustments to have a solid ball-striking day. But if you get too locked in on mechanics at any point in time and feel that it has to be done exactly a certain way, you shut down the Fluid Motion Factor, and playing well becomes an uphill struggle.

In my opinion, golf has gotten too technical. Sophisticated monitoring equipment can measure ball spin rate, club speed, smash factor, carry, launch angle, club delivery and more. Talk about getting your pre-frontal cortex involved! It may very well be beneficial to use all these statistics in the developmental stages of a golfer's career, or when going through a necessary swing change, but there comes a point in time when you should not be captivated by these numbers and instead work on accessing what you already own.

Over the past thirty years the paradigm has shifted from feel to statistics. Byron Nelson, Sam Snead, Ben Hogan, and all the great ball-strikers of past generations didn't have swing coaches following them around from tournament to tournament. They didn't videotape their swings or correct elements of their swing using sophisticated electronic devices. When they had problems with their swings, they went to the range and figured it out—usually by themselves. The best analysis of a swing is ball flight. They adjusted their swings based on feel and that seemed to work well enough.

We all know there are many ways to successfully swing a golf club. Just look at the swings on Tour. But there is only one way the mind produces fluid motion in every swing. The great ball-strikers of past generations instinctively knew this and somehow they got into that space and stayed there the majority of their career. But with all the sophisticated equipment and analysis available in the marketplace today, entry into that space may have become more difficult. When a good swing breaks down the parts of the swing start to be intensely scrutinized. In some ways, it is good that one can see exactly which part of the swing broke down, but in another way, it may not be so beneficial because one can become overly fixated in trying to change it.

When I work with someone and they are not hitting the ball as well as they like, I ignore the swing entirely. I want to water the root first and see what occurs naturally. By watering the root, I am referring to infusing silence into the player's mind and having the parts of the brain that produce motion start working more efficiently. I want to see how much self-correction can occur when this happens. It always amazes me to see how often this sets up a situation that allows the body to self-correct its own mistakes. The problem could be obvious to professional teachers–too steep an angle on the way down or setting it incorrectly at the top, or other mechanical faults. But when the mind is more liquid, the body follows suit and often figures out how to self-correct itself without interference from an outside force—either human or digital. This is an infinitely simpler and more powerful way to correct a swing.

Below is an e-mail I received from Marvol Barnard, a *Golf Digest* Top-50 Teacher, winner of the 2013 Nancy Lopez Golf Achievement award and one of the LPGA teachers I have certified in teaching the Fluid Motion Factor Program that highlights this point:

> So today, I have my last golf lesson of the season, with one of my favorite students who happens to be blind. Dick plays in a lot of the sanctioned tournaments for the blind, here in Arizona and nationally, and I have given him lessons sporadically over the last two years. Dick has three helpers: his wife, and two friends who travel with him to tournaments, put the ball down, aim him properly, etc.

Before I went to the golf course, I was thinking about Dick and his comment to me when I saw him at the range last week when he set up the lesson. He had told me that he is trying to "hit down on the ball," "can't stop 'looking up'" (OMG...really???), and when I exclaimed about both, commented, "I am getting a lot of input from everyone."

I have always felt Dick's fundamentals were sound, and that he IS in fact getting way too much input, from way too many people. Today, I quizzed him about his best rounds, and lo and behold, they are always when his wife is his coach—she knows nothing about golf other than knowing how he should aim. In other words, with her, he is getting no swing advice whatsoever.

We started with a discussion of what "hitting down" really means, versus his understanding of it. We did a little bit of exploration with his wedges, which he is quite good at. I then went right to Ninesville! (Note: "Ninesville" is an integral part of the Fluid Motion Factor Program that allows a golfer to access deeper levels of silence in the pre-shot routine and during the swing. — Author)

The change in his swing was nothing less than remarkable. His helper (one of the "helpful" helpers) was astounded. He had started out the lesson by telling me all that he's "working with" Dick on...keeping his arms close to his body, bending his knee toward the ball in his backswing, keeping his left arm straight...oy vey. No wonder the poor guy was screwed up!

So anyway, where was I? Oh yeah...amazing transformations. He started hitting amazing shots, and could hear and feel the great impact he was making. The pitfall of mood making showed up pretty quick, but he recognized it after coaching, and was able to go back to Ninesville.

I stood there watching this glorious swing appear in front of me... it literally gave me goose bumps and it was over 90 degrees on the range. He hit great shot after great shot. I just stood back and watched genius. Dick's friend was amazed...and quiet. :) He told me when I was leaving that it was the most amazing thing he's ever seen.

That is quite a story.

Usually it is not the swing that is at fault, but the ability to access the swing. The above example highlights that fact. If teachers don't understand those dynamics, and don't give the inner intelligence of the player's body a chance to make the corrections when they are learning, they are reinforcing a less-than-profound paradigm of motion and making it more difficult to make adjustments next time the swing starts to break down.

Better than the most sophisticated of equipment is the inner genius of the body. The players of past generations knew this. They had to move in the direction of that paradigm, because the equipment to analyze swings was just not available. This reinforced the importance of feel and, ultimately, to quicker fixes in their swings. In some ways, too much information could lead to slower fixes when something starts to go astray. Sean O'Hair said he started winning tournaments when he threw away the cameras.

Instead of Tiger being the developmental role model for golfers everywhere, maybe Jack Nicklaus should have that honor. Jack didn't go through four major swing changes like Tiger. He didn't have a swing coach following him around on Tour. Once in a while he would check in with Jack Grout and that would be that. Jack took refuge in the fact that he knew he was going to be able to use his mind (cerebellum) consistently on any given day and adjusted his game accordingly. That was his secret weapon. Because of that, his bad shots were not all that bad.

Think about the best you have ever played. I bet you weren't thinking much about the swing. In fact you probably weren't thinking much about anything. The next day at the range you realized you were doing everything more or less mechanically correct yesterday, so you put all your attention on consciously doing that again and maybe even trying to do it better. Then everything started getting complicated. Maybe you put yourself on a launch monitor, had your swing analyzed from fifteen different angles, got caught up in spin rate and launch angles and before you knew it, you started distancing yourself from using the best weapon in your arsenal—the cerebellum working correctly.

Do you see what is wrong with this picture? Because you have the wrong paradigm about motion, when you play well or play poorly, you return to the surface understanding and ignore the fundamental reason why you have career rounds or career shots or less than desirable rounds. You once again become a prisoner of the swing and try to repeat the swing instead of repeating where the swing originated. How many golfers out there are prisoners of their swing? Way too many. In my mind, there are two reasons for this imprisonment.

The first is that golfers have the wrong paradigm about motion. They have been born in the generation of launch monitors. Because of the abundance of sophisticated tools to analyze swings, golfers have gotten away from figuring things out on their own. They have gotten away from making changes based on feel. It is just too tempting to use the latest and greatest analytical tool to see all the numbers. Because of this dependence, they have moved away from understanding a golf swing from the most fundamental level. That level is the simplicity inherent when someone does play well.

Understanding the simplicity of that level has its challenges. And that leads us to the second reason why golfers have become too much of a prisoner of their swing. Even if they sat down with a neurophysiologist who explained how fluid motion is produced in the body, the ability to repeat that simplicity comes and goes on its own volition and as result, a golfer will most likely take refuge in numbers analysis, rather than a cerebellum analysis. They can change the angle in their swing easier than they can produce silence in their mind. Producing silence is a very delicate task.

But what if all golfers, professionals or amateurs, did what Jack did? What if the millions of golfers throughout the world were able to consistently access the proper functioning of the cerebellum when they play and just let it rip every day? There would probably be more career rounds than one could count and more happy golfers than one could imagine. So the paradigm shift is this:

If it is working most of the time, don't fix it.

Leave your swing alone. Leave it alone if you crush balls on the range, but fail to crush it on the course. The problem is not the swing. The problem lies deeper. The problem is that you are not consistently accessing what you already own. By continually going to the surface level of the problem you are postponing the breakthrough you are waiting for. After enough muscle memory has been established, after a solid swing has been established, processes in the mind are more fundamental than processes in the body. This leads to another paradigm shift.

Golf swings don't win tournaments. It is the ability to access golf swings that wins tournaments.

Let's go back to the range at a PGA tournament. There

are 140 beautiful swings out there. Is there that much difference in those swings? Except for maybe one or two that stand out, probably not. The person who won last week didn't necessarily have the best swing; *for whatever reason they were just able to access their best swing.* The other 139 players couldn't access their best swings consistently and it could have been on just one or two shots. But it was those one or two shots that made the difference between first, second, or fifteenth place.

The ability to access your best swing consistently is the slipperiest of slopes. It is a career-making or career-ending slope. For the golfer in a pressure situation, it is drama to the nth degree. Yet when golfers are able to access what they already own, it feels ridiculously simple. It has to. That feeling of simplicity is a necessity. No one accesses their best swing and says it was a struggle to do so. The repetition of simplicity is the deciding factor in careers, and when golfers understand that crucial point and learn to practice a program to access their swing more consistently, golf will be changed forever. The game will grow exponentially and most golfers will have an excellent chance of reaching their potential.

Chapter 5

Bury It Somewhere in China

The paradigm shifts in this book are counterintuitive. They challenge the status quo of how golfers improve. In the business world, this is known as disruptive technology. Disruptive technology is a term coined by Harvard Business School professor Clayton M. Christensen to describe a new technology that unexpectedly displaces an established technology. In his book, *The Innovator's Dilemma*, Christensen points out that large corporations are designed to work with sustaining technologies. He demonstrates how it is not unusual for a big corporation to dismiss the value of a disruptive technology because it does not reinforce current company goals, only to be blindsided as the technology matures, gains a larger audience, market share, and then threatens the status quo.

The king of disruptive technology was Steve Jobs. He rearranged entire industries with the devices he developed. He rearranged the cell phone industry with the iPhone, the music industry with the iPod and iTunes, and the computer industry with the iMac, MacBook Air, and iPad. When these products appeared in the marketplace, the dominant companies in all these industries were forced to go back to the drawing board to reconfigure and upgrade their products. They had no choice, as Jobs had figured out a better way to do something and the marketplace agreed. He was so contrarian and "disruptive" in his thinking that he never once used consumer focus groups when developing his products, a standard procedure used to gauge consumers' interest and acceptance when new products enter the marketplace. Essentially, he told consumers they needed something they didn't even know they needed and you want to know something—he was right! (I wrote this book on a MacBook Air!)

The "big corporations" in golf are the instructional shows on TV, monthly golf magazine articles, and certification programs for PGA professionals. They represent the status quo in teaching golf. A golf swing in this status quo world is just a combination of right moves or positions that occur during a swing. If you are playing well, you are getting into those positions and if you continually practice getting into those positions, you will play better.

On the one hand, this is a 100% correct understanding of a golf swing. But you now know there are specific reasons why you sometimes get into those positions and sometimes do not. Unless you understand those reasons, your understanding of a golf swing is not complete. This book offers those reasons. This method, in some ways, is in conflict with both the current paradigm of how to accelerate a golfer's progress and the current paradigm of understanding motion. Motion is understood as the right parts being pieced together to form a swing, with a very superficial understanding of why a good swing occurs or breaks down.

On one level, the correct understanding of a golf swing has to do with the parts working correctly. If someone blocks the ball, they probably didn't release the club at impact. If someone slices the ball, either they came across the ball or left the clubface open at impact. But on a more fundamental level, there is a reason why swing mechanics break down. The custodians of the golf status quo may not have this understanding (as of yet!) and that is obvious when you listen to why a golf swing breaks down by the golf pundits on TV. Have you ever heard Nick Faldo or Johnny Miller comment on the failure of the cerebellum to correctly sequence a swing when a golfer blocks their drive?

This is not to say that golf is taught 100% wrong. It is not. For beginning and intermediate students, it is absolutely essential they learn the correct mechanics from a qualified PGA or LPGA professional. And for elite golfers, it is crucial for a qualified instructor to guide them through any swing changes they want to make. There are no shortcuts for this. But once you have practiced enough and enough muscle memory has been established and there is some level of consistency, the paradigm has to change. "Has to" is a strong phrase as it leaves little wiggle room. But laws of motion and how the cerebellum operates are always consistent.

This book is not a discussion of teaching philosophies; it is a description of how the pre-frontal cortex, motor system, cerebellum, and basal ganglia operate to produce fluid motion in a golf swing. Whether you are discussing this with a neurophysiologist from the United States, Australia, England, or Japan, they will all be on the same page—they will explain fluid motion using identical terminology. In many ways, this book does not represent my teaching philosophy or opinion of how to accelerate a student's progress in the game of golf or how to play consistent golf—it represents nature's way. Essentially it is nature's program. It is not a matter of opinion or philosophy as to how the cerebellum operates. The cerebellum operates identically for all golfers. Somehow, those who have broken through in any sport have taken advantage of the genius of the operating system of the muscles and have used the inner intelligence of the body to their advantage; either in competition or when developing their game.

But the ability to access this universal level of intelligence, inherent in every athlete and every golfer to some degree, should not be limited to certain elite golfers; it should be available to all golfers. Until now, there has not been a comprehensive understanding of the parts of the brain physiology responsible for generating fluid motion used in traditional golf instruction or a simple program to access fluid motion consistently. For most players, it has been a hit-or-miss affair, much like rolling dice. Usually, golfers don't know how they are going to play on any given day or why they don't play well. Even the great ones are oftentimes rolling dice, but of course they are very good dice rollers!

Do you think that Tiger, Rory, Phil, or any PGA or LPGA star fully understands how the cerebellum or basal ganglia operate to produce a fluid golf swing? Probably not. In a way, they don't have to. Most of the time, they get the job done. But can you imagine the possibilities if the great players (how about all players!) had a comprehensive understanding of the dynamics that produce fluid motion in a golf swing? It would be exciting to see the results when that happens.

****

Let's return to some more disruptive technology.

There is something I call the DNA Goal in every sport. The DNA Goal is the embedded goal in a sport—meaning you never have to think about it. For instance, when someone shoots a basketball, regardless of what is going on in the game, do you ever have to remind them before they shoot that it would be a good idea if the ball went in the basket? Of course not. It's a DNA Goal.

When someone is about to serve in tennis, regardless of any outside circumstances, either on or off the court, do you have to remind them that it would be a good idea if they got the ball in the service box? Absolutely not. It's a DNA Goal.

Let's return to golf. If someone is on the tee, fairway or green, does anyone ever have to remind them that it would be a good idea if they hit the fairway, hit the green, or sink the putt? Obviously not. They know those are the goals once they start playing the game. But the problem occurs, and it is a huge career-ending problem, when golfers remind themselves once or twice (actually more like six or seven times) to hit the fairway, hit the green, or make the putt. By doing this, by reminding themselves of the obvious, they systematically decrease their chances of executing a motion because they set up a destructive sequence of events in a motion. The destructive sequence is:

- Over-anticipating an action that has not yet occurred.

- Over-anticipation distorts time in the gap—the gap is the moment right before you pull the trigger.

- When time is distorted, when there is a wrinkle in it, the Fluid Motion Factor shuts down.

- When the Fluid Motion Factor shuts down, the bulkier muscles dominate and the motion loses fluidity.

When golfers, or athletes in any sport, remind themselves over and over to execute the DNA Goal, they are doing themselves a disservice and setting up the destructive sequence of events. By reminding themselves of the obvious and not understanding or respecting the delicate nuances of the operating system that produces motion, they are decreasing their chances of executing a successful motion. They are forcing the issue and being too much of a bull in too delicate a china shop.

Everyone has experienced these good and bad dynamics countless times in the course of playing a round of golf. I call the good dynamics the "second shot syndrome." You miss a shot, drop a ball, and hit it perfectly. Or you miss a putt, putt another ball, and drain it. The all-important questions in these two scenarios are where was the DNA Goal on the first shot and where was the DNA Goal on the second shot?

On the first shot the DNA Goal was probably pulsating like the lights outside the Bellagio Hotel in Las Vegas. On the second shot it was probably as dim as lights seen in a snowstorm—there, but in a faint sort of way. On the first shot, you tried to strongly execute the DNA Goal, and therefore it was on the surface level of the mind. On the second shot, the DNA Goal was placed in the proper perspective—more or less hidden from view. That perspective leads us to the paradigm-shifting, disruptive technology concept of:

The goal is not to execute the DNA Goal; the goal is to bury it so it can be executed.

At first glance, this may strike you as something you may not want to do. After all, if you are looking at an eight-foot putt to win a tournament and end up with a career round, why in the world would you not contemplate wanting to make it in any way, shape, or form? Good question. But the real question is not whether you want to make the putt; that answer is obvious. The real question is: *What is the best way to go about it so you give yourself the best chance of making it?* Let's answer that question.

There are three parts to the above paradigm shift. Let's examine them one phrase at a time. We'll start with the middle part: **The goal is to bury it.**

This book could never have been written if the goal on any given golf shot is continually changing. What I mean is, what if all of a sudden golf became much more complicated than it is right now? What if every other fairway you hit, you had to hit it on different sides? Meaning on the first fairway, you had to hit it on the left side, the second fairway you had to hit it on the right side, and the third fairway you had to hit it in the middle. Or when you are putting, what if on the first hole, you had to make the putt in the left side of the cup, the second hole on the right side of the cup and the third hole you had to drain it right in the middle?

Of course this is a ridiculous scenario, but if this was the case, that is, if the DNA Goal was constantly changing and would be easy to forget during a round, then for sure you could not be burying it all the time. If you did that, you might forget what you are supposed to do on the second green or the third fairway.

But that is not the case. It is just the opposite. The DNA Goal on every hole is the same—hit the fairway, hit the green, and sink the putt. But just for safety's sake so you don't lose focus, wouldn't it be a good idea to keep the DNA Goal foremost in your mind so you have a better chance of executing it?

With the understanding you now have of the mechanics of transformations that result in fluid motion, perhaps not. You know there is a certain process that has to occur in the mind in order to produce fluid motion in the body. If this process, the Fluid Motion Factor occurs, the body will be free. If this process does not occur, then regardless of how much focus, concentration, or determination you have, the body will not be free and your chances of a successful outcome diminish significantly. So before the fairway is hit or the putt sunk, the primary goal on any shot is to access the Fluid Motion Factor.

That region of the mind responsible for accessing the Fluid Motion Factor is a delicate one. If it weren't a delicate one, if one could just force the issue, then whoever could force the issue the most, that is, whoever had the strongest will to win, would always access the FMF and come out on top. But that is not the case. There are rules down there. They are subtle and delicate rules, but rules nevertheless. If you understand those rules, those subtle nuances, you have a much better chance of activating the FMF. If you don't understand those rules, or even if you understand them but can't follow them, chances of success decrease.

One very important rule has to do with how much silence you have in your mind right before you begin the motion. Silence is what activates the Fluid Motion Factor. If there is not enough silence, the FMF will shut down. This is one of the main rules of accessing the FMF. Because the DNA Goal can never, ever be forgotten, regardless of the circumstances, the DNA Goal does not have to be on the surface level of the mind when you hit a shot. In fact, if it is too much on the surface level of the mind, quite often you will not experience enough silence for the operating system of the muscles to work efficiently. The brain physiology has certain parameters in order for it to work correctly. These parameters are the same for everyone. If you violate any of the parameters, you will have violated one of the principal rules of the muscle memory bank.

This brings us back to the phrase: **The goal is to bury it.** The only reason the goal is to bury the DNA goal is so more silence can be infused into the mind. The more silence infused into the mind, the better chance you will have of executing the shot because the Fluid Motion Factor will be activated.

Returning to the example of the second shot syndrome, if one reflects on it, there is usually more silence on the second shot than the first. The first shot probably also had more focus than the second. The second shot can be characterized as silence-based and the first shot, focused-based. Major tournament winners live in that second shot silence-based world when they play. They don't have a choice in this, as this is the only way freedom can be produced in a motion.

To give an example of this, let's talk about one of the greatest, if not the greatest putter in the history of the game— Jack Nicklaus. Jack was certainly aware of the DNA Goal in putting. Everyone is aware of the DNA Goal in putting. He didn't have to be reminded that it would be a good idea to make a putt; *everyone* knows it is a good idea to make a putt. But Jack wanted to set up the crucial circumstances so he *could* make a putt. He knew those circumstances were subtle and delicate in nature. He knew that if he didn't set those circumstances up, he would not be able control the line and the speed of the put as well as he would have liked.

Now, of all the great putters in the game, who took the longest over the ball when they putted? Right—Jack. Now what do you think he was thinking about over the ball? I can assure you it was not to remind himself that it would be a good idea to make the putt. In my opinion, he was waiting until the Fluid Motion Factor was activated. He was waiting to activate the quiet process in his mind that would allow him to control the putter and make the putt. If that process took a little longer than most, so be it. He would just wait over the ball until the silence came and only then would he pull the trigger.

David Leadbetter told me that Nicklaus would not pull the trigger until he could visualize the ball going into the hole. This is a very interesting statement since he always took a long time to do that. It doesn't take long when you are over the ball to visualize it going into the hole. This can be done in a second or two. But Jack took more than a second or two over the ball. What then was going on in his mind and what was he waiting for in this visualization process? In my opinion, he was not just visualizing the ball going into the hole, but he was living in the real-time framework of experiencing what his mind had to be experiencing during that visualization process in order to make the putt. He was waiting for the Fluid Motion Factor to kick in. This is a more sophisticated way of visualization and a very subtle point.

There is one thing in visualizing the ball going into the hole. Anyone can do that very quickly when they are over a putt. But Jack's routine wasn't a rote drill of just visualizing the ball going into the hole. He needed to feel exactly how the mind should be functioning in order to access the Fluid Motion Factor right before he pulled the trigger. Jack knew the delicacy of this. He knew that if visualization was done on the surface level of the mind, with the DNA Goal also being on the surface, this was not the most powerful level of visualization and one may be just hoping and wishing the ball goes in.

But visualization done from a quieter, softer level of the

mind, where the Fluid Motion Factor is activated, is the most powerful level of visualization. And oftentimes, the ability to do that operates in its own time frame. You cannot force it and be a bull in a china shop. In other words, you need patience, and Jack had a lot of patience.

You cannot access that silent level of the mind if the DNA Goal is pulsating on the surface level. If the DNA Goal is on the surface level, you will be visualizing the ball going in from the surface level of the mind. This is still visualization, just not the most effective kind. When Nicklaus had a putt he had to make, initially, like everyone else, the DNA Goal was on the surface level when he was over the ball. The DNA Goal is very much like a two-year-old kid who has not eaten all day and you take him to Denny's for dinner. He will constantly be in your face: "Daddy, get me french-fries," "Daddy, get me Coca-Cola," "Daddy, get me ice cream." "*Daddy, make the putt!*"

The kid can't help himself. It is not that he is acting out—after all, he is just a two-year-old kid. Realistically, how do you expect him to act? The DNA Goal is similar. Regardless of how many times you have successfully buried it, it will always be in your face the next shot—especially the next pressure shot. And that is the case even for a player of Jack Nicklaus's status.

So Jack is over the ball to sink a putt to win the U.S. Open or the Masters or any big tournament and that two-year-old kid is in his face and the kid is whining and crying and asking for food, any food, and Jack is just staring the kid down and saying to him: "*I know you are hungry, I know you haven't eaten all day, and I know you can't wait to get some food. But let me just take care of one thing first, and I will give you as much food as you want."* That one thing? Burying the DNA Goal, so he could access the Fluid Motion Factor and make the putt.

A less talented golfer might have pulled the trigger sooner. The DNA Goal and the visualization process would have been on the surface level of the mind; the pressure would have gotten to them and they would have putted. As a result, they may not have accessed the Fluid Motion Factor, which meant the cerebellum could not control the pressure one should have on the club, thereby ensuring a smooth putting stroke and controlling the speed and line of the putt.

But Jack, being Jack, would wait until the cows came home if necessary before he pulled that trigger. He intuitively knew that he if didn't wait until that DNA Goal was buried, he was rolling the dice. He knew if he didn't visualize the ball going into the hole without accessing the Fluid Motion Factor first, he was really rolling the dice and Jack didn't like to roll the dice. So regardless of the situation, regardless if his playing partners were waiting for him to putt, regardless if the spectators were waiting or the TV announcers and TV audience or even the grandmothers at home who never played golf and were just rooting for Jack to make the putt, Jack would not pull the trigger until he was ready. He was going to do it on his clock, not somebody else's and, at the end of the day, he had eighteen major championships under his belt that reflected what a fine timepiece he was always wearing.

But if someone's primary goal is to execute the DNA Goal or visualize the ball going in without first accessing the processes in the mind that will give them a better chance of making it, then the cart is put before the horse. The tail is wagging the dog. Do the muscles control the muscles? No, the mind controls the muscles. Everyone wants to make the putt, but the intelligent approach would be *what do I have to do in order to give myself a better chance of making it?* The analogy would be like trying to get to a specific destination without having a detailed map of how to get there. If someone simply says, "Well just head north for a little while and then go east," that probably won't do the trick.

The DNA Goal is somewhat schizophrenic. On the one hand, it screams out for attention and on the other hand, it knows it can't be fulfilled unless it fades into the background. Like all of us, it has its own battles, but at least it is consistent as it does this on every shot, which means it can be treated with the same process throughout the round. That is fortunate.

****

Let's return to analyzing the other parts of the paradigm-shifting statement: **The goal is not to execute the DNA Goal, the goal is to bury it, so it can be executed.** We have discussed the middle phrase in detail. Let's turn our attention then to the first and third phrases.

"The goal is not to execute the DNA Goal" is like a Zen koan. Remember them? What is the sound of one hand clapping? Of course the goal is to execute it. What other goal is there when you are looking at an eight-foot putt to win the Masters? One has to say that ultimately the goal is to make the putt and if you think there is another goal you are somewhat delusional.

In a way, you are tricking the mind here. But in reality, the mind cannot be tricked. When you think to yourself the goal is not to execute the DNA Goal, you are setting up a confrontation deep inside the mind. You are setting up a competition between believing the goal is not to execute it and the goal is to execute it. The mind has to handle that competition before it can move on to the next intention, which is burying the DNA Goal. In this competition, there will always be one winner. That winner will be the goal is, of course, to execute it.

There is a "fluid cue" I teach that demonstrates what happens when you set up this competition in the mind and when silence is infused in the mind and the DNA Goal is buried. Part of our program revolves around these fluid cues that are done mentally when one swings or putts. One of these fluid cues is having the putt end up in the "general vicinity" of the hole.

When you tell yourself "general vicinity" of the hole, it sets up an interesting scenario in the mind. You have the DNA Goal looking at this idea of general vicinity as if it were an idea from Mars! It says, *What do you mean general vicinity? You can't put a score down for general vicinity; you can only put a score down when you execute me!*

But what happens during the putt, without even knowing it, is you will default to trying to make the putt, even though your goal will be the general vicinity of the hole. You can't help yourself with this. But having the idea of general vicinity will soften the effect the DNA Goal has on your mind. It will infuse more silence in your mind, which will give you a better chance of executing the DNA Goal.

Softening the DNA Goal will always give you a better chance of making the putt.

Regardless of what you tell yourself to do in regard to the DNA Goal, you always want to execute it. Even when you tell yourself to bury it, in the back of your mind as you are burying it, you know you want to execute it. You can't really fool yourself about that. So as you are burying it, you know it has to be executed, so in a way that is why you can bury it in the first place! I may be splitting hairs here, but these are the subtle dynamics that automatically take place in the minds of great putters.

Which brings us to the final phrase: **so the putt can be executed.** That is the ultimate goal. That will always be the winner in the competition between burying the DNA Goal and making the putt. The fact is that no matter where the DNA Goal is buried, Beijing if you live in New York or New York if you live in Beijing, you will always want to make the putt. When you tell someone to bury a thought, you are telling them not to think about it and not to let it have any influence in their actions.

You just can't do that with the DNA Goal. It is too radioactive and its half-life is a billion years! Meaning that regardless of where it is buried in your mind, it will be pulsating in your awareness somewhere. By burying it, by softening the effect it has in your mind, you are helping to trigger the mechanics that will give you the best chance of making it. Ironically, the DNA Goal will always be winking at you on the way down as you bury it and thinking:

"Fine. Bury me in China or New York—I don't have a problem with that. Bury me in the furthest part of the

galaxy—I don't have a problem with that either. I know what you are doing and I know regardless of where you bury me, I know your true intentions, which is to execute me. So play your little games here and let's see who has the last laugh."

That conversation should take place on every shot on the course. The same dynamics apply: bury the DNA Goal so you have a better chance of executing it. Bury the DNA Goal so the Fluid Motion Factor can be activated. Though it may sound counterintuitive, it reflects the deepest wisdom you can have. Just think of your career rounds. They were a result of the subtle parts of the operating system of the muscles working correctly. It felt simple, effortless, and automatic because the DNA Goal was buried. Great putters and ball strikers are permanent residents in that special world.

Chapter 6

Weekly Drawings

Bill Haas had a three-shot lead going into the final round of the 2013 Northern Trust Open at Riviera in Los Angeles. After his spectacular seven-under-65 third round, he was asked a question that just about every professional golfer and for that matter, every golfer usually ask themselves every time they play: *"What swing thought will you have tomorrow?"*

Swing thoughts. Swing keys. They are the Holy Grail of golf. They keep the golf magazines in business. They have made Michael Breed a superstar. They keep you coming back to the Golf Channel, as you are eternally optimistic that one day, somebody will say something that just makes perfect sense and so perfectly suited to your game, that finally you will have a lifeboat that will take you across the River Jordan to the Promised Land and you will live there peacefully, with a lower handicap, and no three-putts, forever. And for most golfers, these swing thoughts change week to week and round to round.

Unfortunately, the swing thought for Bill Haas didn't work in the final round. His swing thought was not to get ahead of the ball on the way down. On Sunday, he shot a three-over 73 and finished tied for third. But there have been days when Bill's swing thoughts worked spectacularly well. One of those days was in the final round of the Fed-Ex Cup in 2011, when he won $11.2 million and the title.

Why do swing thoughts work? Why do they sometimes not work? Before answering those questions, let's ask another question: Why do you often have your best rounds with no swing thoughts? Golfers always want to repeat their best performance. There are usually a few characteristics associated with those career rounds—a feeling of effortlessness, simplicity, fluidity, and oftentimes, no swing thoughts.

On your best ball-striking days, the mind's path to the basal ganglia had no roadblocks. Think of it like driving on a superhighway in the early morning hours—no traffic, no delays, and very quickly arriving at your destination. This is the ideal scenario whenever you drive on that road. And similarly, when you played your best golf, there were no obstacles in accessing the muscle memory you had in the bank. You had an intention and then consistently executed it.

The reason why the path was so effortless that day has its origin in the laws of physics. Physics explains how the universe operates. Since we are very much a part of the universe, it also explains how we operate. One of the most universal laws in the universe is the law of least action. Nature always performs the least amount of work to get the job done. She is supremely efficient. That is why when something is dropped, gravity figures out the shortest path for it to travel to the ground. Or when shining a light beam between two mirrors, the light beam always travels the shortest path between them. These are very obvious and common sense examples of the law of least action, but they clearly indicate its ubiquity.

We are also part of nature and the law of least action operates within us as well. For a golf swing, that means we swing best when the least amount is going on in our mind. Then the Fluid Motion Factor is accessed and the body is free to do what it knows best to do. And it figures out how to do that in the simplest possible manner.

Which leads us back to swing thoughts. With enough practice, when enough muscle memory has been developed and the law of least action kicks in, the mind and the body want to follow the path of least resistance. If given the opportunity, the body always wants to default to the simplest mode of operation during a golf swing. Only when it defaults to its simplest mode of operation will it be able to access the muscle memory bank and allow for consistent play. Playing exceptional golf always feels simple and you never get simplicity from complexity, so the mind has to feel like it is operating simply in order to play well.

If there are any unnecessary levels of thought involved in trying to access what you already own, you will have violated a subtle principle of the law of least action. This is the reason you usually have no swing thoughts, or swing thoughts that are very faint in your awareness when you play your best golf. In a sense when you go 'unconscious' or play 'out of your mind,' you are using the mind the way it is supposed to be used. The instructional manual of how the mind operates when playing exceptional golf always reads the same: how little can you do mentally during a motion and still have it be effective? Then the body feels like it is has been let out of prison and the swing is most effective.

That is not to say that someone cannot play exceptional golf while having swing thoughts. There have obviously been countless tournaments won throughout the world with the winning player having them. For many players, not to have them would be an unnatural situation and anytime there is an unnatural situation created in the mind, it will not be good. But there is a way to have swing thoughts that will not violate any of the subtle nuances of the law of least action and that leads to excellent results. In other words, it is possible to have swing thoughts and still have the mind operate in its simplest possible mode. That is a delicate process, but very doable. This is how it works.

The mind is like an ocean. There are surface, active levels and there are softer, quieter levels. Everyone has experienced these levels many times during the course of a day. The mind can be very active at work, and on the way home (as long as there is no traffic!), the mind often settles down and reflects on the events of the day. Another time the mind settles down is when we close our eyes for sleep waiting for the Feather Ball Express to pick us up.

When the mind settles down, it starts to incorporate the principles of the law of least action and by so doing, becomes more powerful. How many times have we tried to solve a problem or sticky situation during the day, failed to come up with a solution and out of the blue, the solution appears as we are falling asleep. Why? Because when the mind settles down, it becomes more integrated and is able to analyze and interpret events from a more powerful, abstract level.

If the mind can access deeper levels on the way to sleep, it can also access deeper levels during a golf swing. And this ability to access deeper levels results in Masters and U.S. Open victories. In fact, this is the main reason why someone wins those tournaments. Remember Tiger's statement, "I took the club out of the bag and I didn't remember anything until I saw the ball land on the green." Did his mind become dull or lethargic when this occurred? Just the opposite—it was living and breathing in the land of least action, the most powerful space in the universe to produce effective motion.

Just as there are surface and quieter levels of the mind, one can say there are similar levels in the body. The body has the bulkier, core muscles, which can represent the surface level of the body's structure. It also has the fast-twitch muscles, as well as the inherent ability for the body to self-correct during a motion. Though the bulkier muscles are important in a motion, if they dominate, the motion will not be effective. When the fast-twitch muscles fire in the right sequence, balls explode off drivers and irons are hit crisper. Now here is the crucial point.

When intentions are generated from the surface level of the mind, only the bulkier muscles can be activated. But when intentions are generated from softer, quieter levels of the mind, a deeper level of intelligence is activated in the body that allows for correct sequencing in a motion.

Mind	Body
Surface, active levels	Gross, bulkier muscles

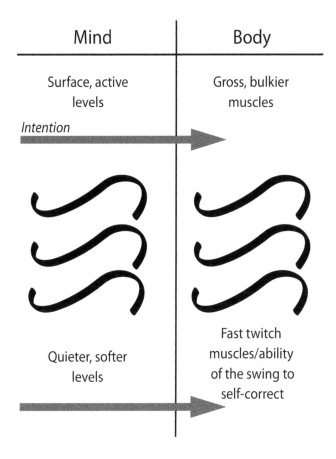

Intention

Quieter, softer levels	Fast twitch muscles/ability of the swing to self-correct

This is the reason why swings look fluid one day and out of sequence another day. When someone is not swinging well, they are generating their intentions from surface levels of the mind and as a result, not accessing the deeper levels of intelligence in the mind and body. But when swing thoughts are generated from quieter levels, they automatically have access to the deeper levels of intelligence in the body. Much more important than the swing thought is where the thought originated. If it were simply the swing thought, then you would never let go of that swing thought your whole career.

But even professional golfers change swing thoughts and they change them a lot. They work great one week and not so great the next. Why?

Because when a swing thought dominates the awareness and is generated from the surface level of the mind, the correct sequencing and energy flow during the swing is restricted and the swing has less chance of being effective. This prevents the fast-twitch muscles from firing. The consequences of this will be having the wrong parts of the swing dominating at the wrong time, such as holding on to the club at impact or increasing the tempo.

But when swing thoughts are generated from quieter levels of the mind, the swing has a greater chance of being successful. It wants to live in that quiet space during a swing. It knows it can produce the best results when it is in that space. But through a lifetime of not understanding motion, golfers lose their ability to live in that space. Here are two reasons why:

1. Golfers have been taught that more focus, more determination, and more concentration will produce better results. That is just not so. Better results only occur when the Fluid Motion Factor is accessed. The Fluid Motion Factor can only be accessed within a very subtle framework, which oftentimes golfers do not know how to consistently access. Golfers can always have more focus, work harder, and be more determined, but accessing the Fluid Motion Factor marches to the beat of a different drummer. So golfers usually default to more focus when the pressure is on, rather than more silence. Tiger has reinforced that direction countless times on TV. A whole generation has grown up

watching him stalk a putt or execute an iron shot with steely determination and an icy "I am going to get the job done at all costs" kind of stare.

But remember what his inner experience was on key shots in major tournaments. On one level he may look super-determined, but on another, more fundamental level, he has the innocence of a child during a motion, especially when putting. Remember his statement, "I took the club out of the bag and I didn't remember anything until I saw the ball land on the green." That is 180 degrees from no pain, no gain. On the outside he looks like a tiger stalking his prey, but on the inside his mind is operating from the level of the law of least action. That is one of the main reasons he dominated golf for so long. It was not so much the quality of his swing that defined his career, as it was the quality of his silence.

2. Most golfers have an incomplete understanding of motion. They understand motion as a series of movements that have to be pieced together to form a whole. The more they practice those movements, the better they will become. On one level, this understanding of motion is 100% correct—the club has to adhere to specific geometrical and physics principles to execute a shot. In many ways, a golf swing is based on the laws of physics. But we know there are many "certain ways" that are acceptable. Because of this incomplete understanding of motion, golfers tend to overemphasize one part of the swing to the detriment of the wholeness of the swing, thinking if they can just get the club or the body in one position, everything else will fall into place like a row of dominos and they will have an excellent chance of hitting a

solid shot. This over-focus on the parts of the swing shuts down the brain from operating in the manner needed to play consistently.

That kind of thinking is not the most profound way to understand motion. Ultimately, what everyone is trying to do when swinging well is simply to access the muscle memory they already have in the bank. That's it. If they can do that, they have accomplished their task. That is when all the parts of the swing will be working together like a finely-tuned orchestra. Now here is the fact that may make golf instructors rethink their approach to the game. There are only two ways you cannot access the muscle memory in your account. The first is if the Fluid Motion Factor shuts down. The second is:

If any part of the motion or the shot overshadows the wholeness of the motion, you will have difficulty in accessing your muscle memory.

This is a game-changing statement for every sport. This means if you have a swing thought during a motion that overshadows the wholeness of the motion, you will not have full access to your funds. But we know that most golfers put most of their eggs in the basket of having the right swing thought. They wake up the morning before a round and make a commitment to that thought. They think about that thought on the way to the course and when they are on the range warming up. They use that swing thought during a round as a lifeline that will allow them to play well. On one hand, that commitment may be justified because when they do execute that swing thought, things usually work out.

But it would be extremely useful to understand why on two shots, with identical swing thoughts, one shot worked and the other didn't. You can't blame the swing thought because they were identical on both shots. This clearly indicates that having the right swing thought does not necessarily mean it will result in a good shot. *It is not so much the swing thought, as it is where the swing thought was generated from which determines the success of the shot.* The swing thought must be generated from a quieter level of the mind so as not to overshadow the wholeness of the swing.

The first two or three feet of taking the club back are crucial for this. If in those first two or three feet, the wholeness of the motion is lost, then regardless of having the perfect swing thought, chances of success diminish. Those first few feet of the swing are the moment of truth. If a part of the swing or a goal of the shot dominates too much, the Fluid Motion Factor will not be accessed. The first two or three feet in the takeaway are where careers and career shots are formed. But we are made to believe in articles we read or in the TV we watch that certain parts of the swing executed correctly are the crucial elements in producing a good swing. When Tiger's, or Rory's, or Phil's or anybody's swing on Tour breaks down, we are led to believe it is because some part of the swing broke down.

On one level, it is absolutely true that a swing breaks down because certain positions were not achieved during the swing. But a more fundamental question that should be asked is, "Why were those positions achieved on some shots and not others?" If one becomes fixated on getting into particular positions and understands the swing will only work if those positions are achieved, then one can get lost in the parts of the swing for a very long time and not understand the crucial significance of experiencing the wholeness of the swing in the takeaway. This lack of understanding is a less-than-profound way of understanding motion and has stunted the careers of many professional and amateur golfers and in fact has caused many players to give up the game.

Though it is necessary to understand the mechanics of a swing, knowledge of correct mechanics do not necessarily translate into more consistency. Pick up any golf magazine and you will see the swing dissected innumerable ways. This is reinforcing the paradigm of understanding a swing in terms of parts. Even when someone is learning the game, *especially when someone is learning the game*, the swing has to be understood in terms of wholeness. If it is not, then throughout a golfer's career, they will be practicing and understanding a swing in terms of parts and will not make as much progress as they could if they understood it in terms of wholeness.

If at any point in the swing, the Fluid Motion Factor is not accessed, then you run the risk of not accessing your muscle memory or of having the body's ability to self-correct itself during a swing. Any point means exactly that—any point. Everything may look good in a swing right up until the moment of impact, but if the Fluid Motion Factor is not accessed then, the cerebellum will not be able to self-correct any faults that may occur at impact, such as leaving the club-face open or not releasing properly. This means that wholeness has to be experienced at every point in the swing.

This is not to say that one cannot think about a part of the swing during the swing, it just means the thinking of that part cannot overshadow experiencing the swing in terms of wholeness. When a good swing breaks down, it just meant that wholeness broke down.

Because everyone's operating system of the muscles works identically, whether it is Tiger's, yours, or mine, everyone has to understand and practice motion from this perspective of wholeness. A golf swing also has to be taught, repeated and commented on from this perspective. Unfortunately, that is not the case. This is not to say that one should not work on a specific part of the swing when developing their game. At times it is absolutely necessary to go in there and work on changing something. But there is a very effective way to change a swing. That way is very simple: When you go in there and do corrective surgery, while you are working on the parts, never lose sight of the whole. The wholeness of the swing has to be in the forefront at all times.

Changing parts of your swing is similar to a potter molding clay. What is the first thing a potter does when he wants to mold clay? He moistens it. He has to moisten it because if he doesn't, when he tries to shape it into different forms, the clay will resist and, because of its brittleness, may break. In trying to change your swing, you are asking your body to get into positions it is not used to getting into. Therefore it may initially resist that change. The golfer has to be like the intelligent potter and "moisten" the mind. This means making the mind malleable and flexible by infusing it with silence. If you ask the body to get into a new position without first infusing silence into the mind, it may resist the change. The mind is so deeply connected to the body that if the mind does not become flexible first, the body will not either.

In order to do that, you must generate the intention of changing a part of the swing from a softer and quieter level of the mind. You should be thinking as if you are tiptoeing in the room of an infant sleeping and you do not want to wake the baby up. It has to feel very delicate and innocent, with only a slight intention to change some aspect of your motion. And of course the wholeness can never be lost in your awareness. This method will accelerate the process and also make it more resilient when you are in competition.

The first goal of any swing thought should be to trigger the Fluid Motion Factor and then have an effect on a part of the swing. If the attention is so caught up in the swing thought and becomes a prisoner of it, then you are violating an aspect of how the operating system of the muscles works. It may then be challenge to have a consistent swing, especially under pressure situations, where everything is accentuated.

In 1945, Byron Nelson won eleven tournaments in a row. During that stretch he said he didn't practice much. When asked why, he said: "I don't want to lose the feel I have right now." Interesting comment. Why he did say that and why do golfers consistently change swing thoughts? Here is my take on that.

A successful swing thought produces a kinesthetic feel in the body. That feel is golden as it allows the swing to be sequenced correctly. Essentially it allows someone to access the Fluid Motion Factor. But because we are always looking for patterns in the universe, we start to get enamored with that feel, because it is allows us to play better golf. Eventually that feel overshadows the ability to experience the shot in terms of wholeness, a necessary prerequisite to accessing the Fluid Motion Factor and accessing your best swings. The swing then starts to break down. The swing thought stops working, so you search for another swing thought and another feel and start the whole process again.

Byron found the right feel associated with the right swing thought. He didn't have to practice it because he already knew it worked. Had he practiced it, it probably would have started to become the star of the show and overshadow the wholeness of the swing. Good thinking. The result? Eleven in a row.

And finally, I want to plant a seed in your mind. Ask yourself this question: When you played your best golf, did you have any swing thoughts? I would imagine many of you would say no. That slippery slope of accessing your muscle memory was not so slippery that day. In fact it was just the opposite—it felt very easy to access what you already owned. If, when you played your best golf you didn't have any swing thoughts, or the swing thoughts were very soft, they were hardly there at all, why aren't you trying to set up that condition all the time?

Chapter 7

A Walk in the Park

Every golfer takes a little walk when they play. The walk I am referring to is not the walk between shots, but the walk one takes from behind the ball to the ball to hit a shot. In my opinion, those walks are the most important walks, in fact, the most important *anything* a golfer does during a round. The quality of those walks and what takes place during them will greatly determine how you play. Let me explain.

By now you understand that once you have established enough muscle memory, your goal when playing is to access what you already own. When that occurs, you will be able to squeeze everything you can out of your round. Everything you do when you play should be geared to accomplishing that goal. This *especially includes* the walk into the shot. That walk begins the moment of truth in hitting a golf shot.

Everything done in those few steps should be helping you access what you already own. Unfortunately, for many golfers, the opposite is true. What they experience in that walk oftentimes moves them farther away from playing consistently.

The typical scenario when setting up a shot is this; you stand behind the ball and determine what shot you want to hit. You take into consideration all the factors surrounding the shot: target, wind, lie, shape of the shot, club selection, where you stand in the round, and other factors. Once a shot has been decided, you start your walk.

During that walk most golfers are very focused on what they want to do. Very focused. They think the more they focus, the more they remind themselves of all the elements of the shot, especially the target, the better the chance of executing it. After all, you do not get many chances in golf, and one bad swing in a round can be the turning point. So on every shot, one better stay focused, pay attention and make it count. The only problem with this mind-set, which is this typical over-focused mind-set of golfers, is with every step they take toward the ball, they are often times decreasing their chances of hitting a good shot.

Here is a perfect example. Say you are 150 yards from the green and your normal 150-yard shot is a seven iron. You take your club out of the bag, stand behind the ball, and start zeroing in on your target. You quickly realize the wind has died down and the pin is in the middle of the green. You immediately see this as an ideal seven iron and you visualize the shot.

Now here is a very simple, but highly significant question

that every golfer should ask themselves about any shot they are about to hit: Under any circumstance, regardless of what is going on in the round, or for that matter, what is going in any aspect of your life, after you have visualized the shot, are you going to forget you are 150 yards away from the pin and this is a seven iron for you? This begs another important question: Why then do most golfers in this kind of situation remind themselves three, four or sometimes ten times of what they want to do on any given shot?

The less-than-profound reason of why they remind themselves of the shot over and over again is either:

- They were taught to do that.

- They want to hold on to something they think will give them a better chance of hitting it well.

See the shot, feel the shot, hit the shot. And see and feel the shot as many times as you can. But continuously holding on to visualizing the shot can systematically shut down the Fluid Motion Factor. It can make you a prisoner of that visualization. That thought becomes so predominant in your mind as you are walking into the shot that it wakes up the pre-frontal cortex and keeps it awake on the way to the ball, over the ball and most likely when you pull the trigger. In reality, you are continuously reminding yourself of the obvious and that often has a very detrimental effect in being able to access what you already own because it blocks the pathway to your muscle memory in the basal ganglia and clogs the circuitry in the mind in an instant.

Once you stand behind the ball and see that it is a seven-iron shot and you visualize the shot, are you ever going to forget that fact? No. Are you going to ever forget that fact in the three or four seconds it takes to walk to the ball and the other seven or eight seconds it takes to hit the shot? Of course not. Then why would you continually remind yourself of the obvious? There is no good reason to do that. Once the shot has been visualized, you are not going to forget what you want to do, so why not make that walk into the shot a walk that will trigger accessing the Fluid Motion Factor and your muscle memory, instead of reminding yourself of the obvious over and over again.

You can access the Fluid Motion Factor more consistently by visualizing the shot and then burying that visualization— just the opposite of what most people do. This will give you a better chance of accomplishing what you want to do on any shot, which is accessing what you already own. It will start to infuse more silence in the mind and greatly decrease the drama associated with hitting a shot. The purpose of the pre-shot routine (which I would like to rename the Fluid Motion Preparation!) should be threefold:

1. Accessing the Fluid Motion Factor.

2. Creating the correct algorithm–a seed that contains the wholeness of the shot.

3. Making sure that seed does not get corrupted at any point in time.

When you stand behind the ball and determine what kind of shot you want to hit, you immediately create an algorithm. An algorithm is a mathematical formula that contains a step-by-step procedure to solve a problem. For instance, Google uses an algorithm to determine which sites show up on the first page of any particular search. Let's say you want to look for golf courses in Orlando. You type in Orlando golf courses and, believe it or not, 11,400,000 results come up! That is because every URL or every site that contains the words "Orlando," "golf," or "course" shows up on the search. Showing up on the first page of a search is the goal of every website and is achieved through a top-secret algorithm that Google uses. The algorithm would seek out parameters such as how many of the words in your search show up on a site, how long the site has been up, how many links there are to the site and other factors.

When you stand behind the ball you create an algorithm for that shot which contains all the elements necessary to execute it. This includes how the body feels when it hits the shot, where and how you want to hit it and every other factor surrounding the shot. The algorithm is like a seed that contains the wholeness of what you want to do and how you want to do it. Once that algorithm, or seed, is created, you can never forget it. That is the beauty of the algorithm and that is why once you create it, you can forget about it because it will always be with you. It is like the DNA Goal of the shot, the imbedded goal, and something that can never be forgotten. Bury it as deeply as you want because the deeper you bury it, the better chance you have of executing it. This is counterintuitive, but true.

At any point in time during the Fluid Motion Preparation the algorithm can get corrupted. There are innumerable ways it can get corrupted. For instance, if one is thinking over and over about what has to be done in the shot, it usually gets corrupted. It no longer contains the wholeness of the shot, but is just a collection of parts where one part overshadows the wholeness—don't hit it left, don't hit it right, don't hit it long, don't hit it short, etc. When you create an algorithm, all these factors have been automatically computed. When you remind yourself of these factors, the path to the basal ganglia is like a traffic jam on a highway. You are telling yourself way too many times in the Fluid Motion Preparation about the conditions already inherent in the algorithm. Then, when you pull the trigger, you are more or less rolling the dice on the shot because the circuitry of the brain physiology has been clogged.

A student of mine, who is an excellent golfer and who once caddied for Nick Price, told me a story about Nick that exemplifies this point. As most people know, Nick played rather quickly. He saw the shot, walked up to the ball, and pulled the trigger. During his prime, no one was a better ball-striker than Nick. In fact he is considered one of the best ball-strikers of all time. Nick wanted my student to know his routine when he played. In his routine, he would stand behind the ball, visualize the shot, walk into the shot, and then he would not think about what he wanted to do with the ball ever again. He told his caddy: "*Why would I want to remind myself of hitting a high cut when I am over the ball and about to swing? I already knew I wanted to do that when I stood behind the ball and figured out what shot I wanted to hit. I already know how to hit a high cut and reminding myself of the obvious is not going to increase my chances of executing it.*"

Point well made.

Nick did not have to remind himself of what he wanted to do with the shot. That was created in a few seconds when he stood behind the ball. He certainly wasn't going to forget it on the way to the ball or when he stood over the ball and was about to pull the trigger. Intuitively, he knew if he reminded himself of the obvious, he would decrease his chances of executing the shot. He wanted to do everything within his power to hit a good shot and execute the algorithm and this included, *especially included*, not reminding himself of it.

The walk into the shot and the time over the shot are the crucial elements in determining how you play on any given day. The purpose of that walk should be to access the Fluid Motion Factor. When that occurs, you have a much better chance of setting up the conditions of accessing what you already own. Ideally, the mind should be getting quieter and quieter with every step. When you are over the ball, the quality of what you are experiencing gets even more important until that moment in time when you are about to pull the trigger. The importance of how you are thinking (not what you are thinking) right before you pull the trigger is the most overlooked element in all of golf. THAT is the moment of truth—the moment that more or less will determine how you hit the shot.

What the mind is experiencing right before you pull the trigger most likely will be what the mind will be experiencing during the shot. The reason is there may not be enough time during the swing to experience anything else. Everything is happening too quickly. If the Fluid Motion Factor is accessed right before the trigger is pulled, it will usually be accessed during the shot. If it is not accessed then, it becomes an uphill struggle to access it during the swing. Well begun is half done. In fact it is much more than half done.

The most overlooked element in golf is the quality of time right before you swing. It determines tournament winners at all levels of the game. By quality of time, I am referring to time either moving normally, as it is as you are reading this sentence, or time that has a "wrinkle" in it. By wrinkle I am referring to time either being frozen, stuck in the past, or over-anticipating an action that has not yet occurred. This immediately sets up the destructive sequence in any motion. The Fluid Motion Factor then shuts down and the bulkier, core muscles dominate the swing.

In regards to this, there is something I call fluidity of thinking. Fluidity of thinking means that your thoughts are moving like a river. When this occurs, the body is free. But if your thoughts are frozen in time or too much in the past or future, the body is not free. Most poor shots have their origin in the quality of thinking right before the swing starts. So in a very real way, that moment right before you pull the trigger is more important than the actual swing. If there is an imbalance then, most likely there will be an imbalance during the swing. By the time the swing starts, the ship is already headed out to sea and the direction is set. You want to make sure you do everything within your power to ensure that it is heading in the right direction. Otherwise, in the immortal words of one of my favorite songs by Carole King, "It's Too Late Baby!"

How do you know you are experiencing that moment correctly? How can you better ensure you have fluidity of thinking over the ball? What is the litmus test? Here is a good one.

On the range, visualize yourself about to hit an important shot during the round. Go through your normal pre-shot routine (Fluid Motion Preparation!) and get over the ball. Now right before you pull the trigger, drop the club and stand up. If you felt there was a big contrast of what you experienced when you stood up versus what you experienced when the club was in your hands right before you pulled the trigger, then you are behind the eight ball even before you swing. If there is a big contrast, that is, you feel much freer and lighter, then the Fluid Motion Factor has shut down. By contrast, I am referring to how you feel inside—whether there was more anxiety, apprehension, fear, or just an overall nervous feeling.

There will always be a contrast when the club is in your hand versus when it is not in your hands over the ball. When there is a club in your hand, you can hit a ball and when there is no club in your hand, you obviously cannot. But if there is a big contrast, you are at a distinct disadvantage. It means there is too much "drama" occurring and most likely you will not have fluidity of thinking. It will then be an uphill struggle to access what you already own. If there is just a slight contrast, which means the Fluid Motion Factor has been accessed, then chances are the brain will continue to access the Fluid Motion Factor during the swing and your chances of hitting a good shot greatly increase. When there is very little contrast between the club in your hands and out of your hands, I call this Setting One, One being the time right before you pull the trigger.

Everything you do in the Fluid Motion Preparation, *everything*, should be done with the goal of Setting One. If anything is done that takes away from achieving that goal, you are doing yourself a great disservice. But most golfers, in my opinion, systematically do things in the Fluid Motion Preparation that significantly decrease their chances of Setting One correctly. These include:

- Reminding themselves of the algorithm
  continuously on the way to the ball and over the ball.

- Reminding themselves of some elements of the
  swing they want to do correctly.

- Reminding themselves of the DNA Goal.

All this reminding significantly decreases your chances of playing well. Do you remind yourself that it would be a good idea to drive on the right side of the road when you drive? If you want to remind yourself of something when you play, remind yourself of how little you reminded yourself of anything when you played your best.

When One is set correctly, the inner intelligence of the body takes over when you swing. Think of it like this; when you go to an ATM machine and insert your card and then enter your pin to get your $20, do you really care what levers are used and in what order they are used to give you that $20? Of course not. Think of Setting One like entering your debit card into an ATM machine. You do it and then let the machine do its thing.

But if the drama builds with every step you take towards the ball in the Fluid Motion Preparation, like you are getting on a bus to go to a war zone (Okay, that may be a little exaggerated, but you see the point), then by the time you arrive at the ball and set the club behind it, you are significantly decreasing your chances of accessing the Fluid Motion Factor. The walk toward the ball should be like the walk from one room in your house to another—straightforward and with one purpose: to arrive in the next room with as little fanfare as possible. It should be like the walk you take from one aisle in Wal-Mart to another aisle. Or the walk you take from the parking lot to the clubhouse. No drama there.

Certainly there are situations where that walk does contain some drama. Those are the situations where you are either in between clubs or in between shot selections or have a key shot in the round or in the case of putting, not too sure of the speed or the line. In every round you are going to be faced with these situations. When you have a challenging situation or are undecided, you create an algorithm, just as you create one for every other situation. But because of indecision, the algorithm is underdeveloped. This underdeveloped algorithm stands on shaky ground. You have not entrusted it with any significant power, just like a building with a shaky foundation can sway too much in the wind because of an insecure foundation. Therefore, when you try to Set One with this algorithm, it becomes challenging, if not impossible, to do. If someone took the club out of your hand just before you initiated the swing with an underdeveloped algorithm, you would definitely feel a contrast.

The shot then becomes iffy. It may or may not work.

These situations appear in every round. What can you do to prevent them from happening? You should know that Setting One will always be very challenging on five or six shots in every round. Be prepared to handle them in an intelligent way when they do appear. By an intelligent way, always know you have the option of backing away when you are over the ball if you feel One has not been set correctly. Backing off shows strength. It shows that you understand the most important element of the shot, which is the quality of what you are experiencing right before you pull the trigger and that you are able to make changes on the fly. That ability could save the round or win the tournament for you.

An excellent way to make Setting One a habit is to do it when you practice. Evaluate every shot on a scale of 1–10, not by the quality of the shot, but by how well One is set. In a very short period of you will see the relationship between how well One is set and the quality of the shot. By practicing like this, you will start culturing in your mind the importance of Setting One and eventually it will become a habit when you play.

Another way of Setting One correctly is to practice what I call the Universe drill. When you stand behind the ball in the pre-shot routine, you immediately create an algorithm. Let's call the space you do this in Universe One. As soon as the algorithm is created, you walk towards the ball. Let's call the space around the ball Universe Two. Ideally, as soon as the algorithm is created, not only should it be buried, but also Universe One should be 'destroyed' because you will never forget its content. Imagine Universe One and Universe Two are lakes. What normally happens when one crosses into Universe Two is that the information from Universe One is continually flowing into Universe Two, much like a tributary connecting two lakes.

This has the effect of reminding you of the obvious and minimizing your chances of accessing the Fluid Motion Factor. The purpose of Universe One is to create the algorithm. When you step into Universe Two, the purpose is to forget what you created in Universe One, Set One and access the Fluid Motion Factor. If you do that, you greatly increase your chances of hitting the shot you want. Understanding the Fluid Motion Preparation as a crucial, if not the most crucial, element in playing well will go a long way in making you a more consistent golfer and reaching your full potential as a golfer.

Chapter 8

The Origin of the Program

In 1971, I was the Florida State High School singles tennis champion and a member of the championship team. I had a very good college career at the University of Pennsylvania playing #1 singles. I was a member of the All-Ivy team one year and even had a win over John McEnroe in a dual match. But by the time I was a senior at Penn, I was burned out on tennis. I had played two to three hours every day since I was thirteen and, as the saying goes, "The thrill was gone."

But then something magical happened that changed my life.

In an intra-squad challenge match, I had an extraordinary Zone experience. Three things happened to me that are the characteristics of all Zone experiences:

1. Time slowed down.

2. My mind became very quiet.

3. My motion became effortless and super-fluid.

I walked off the court in a daze. I felt like I had just been in a Walt Disney movie, where an ordinary Joe walks off the street, becomes a superhero for a couple of hours, and then returns to his day job. I sat down, trying to capture all my thoughts and feelings, because at the tender age of twenty-two, I knew this was an experience that was going to change my life. I knew I had to fully understand what happened because the feeling associated with this experience was very much spiritual in nature and my major in college was religion. I felt expanded and not attached to my actions in the least—as if an outside force was in charge and I was just a bystander watching the action unfold.

After two days of reflection, I realized what precipitated the experience. I had taken lessons from some of the top teachers in the country, but nobody ever came close to teaching me the reason why I went into the Zone that day. In our first book, *The 7 Secrets of World Class Athletes*, I go into great detail about Zone experiences and why they occur. That book and why I had my Zone experience can be summarized in one sentence:

The quality of silence changed.

The quality of silence changed as I was waiting for the ball in a rally and that triggered the Fluid Motion Factor. It allowed my body to be free to perform at the highest possible level. It was as if I understood the great secret of sports and, since sports were such a huge part of my life, I felt a deep sense of fulfillment inside. I had competed in so many tournaments over a ten-year period, played so many matches, walked off the court with such diverse emotions that the realization that tennis matches are decided by qualities of silence was an epiphany for me.

I now understood that matches were decided in the 'Gap,' the period of time after you hit a shot and are waiting to hit the next one. When this below-the-radar, two-to-three seconds of time changes, the match changes. And by change, I refer to the quality of silence one experiences during this period of non-motion. It becomes more refined and more powerful. Ultimately, the quality of the Gap determines the quality of the motion. Coaches, players, commentators are all concerned about the quality of the motion, but I realized they didn't understand that by the time you got to the motion, it was already too late, the ship was out to sea and the direction the boat was heading was 100% determined in the Gap.

I knew I was investigating a very subtle and not fully understood area in sports and in my twenty-two-year-old-I-can-do-anything-very-fast naïveté, I thought it would take a year or two to develop a program to teach someone to have more silence when they played. After all, the whole feeling was so simple when it happened to me (and when it happens to anyone) that I thought it shouldn't be that difficult to figure out.

I was a little off in the time calculations. It took thirty-seven years.

It took that long because to infuse silence in the mind is

the most delicate of tasks. Though the mind operates best when silence is present, the pressure inherent in sports and the sheer dynamism of movement often prevent silence from being present. One has to be very cognizant and knowledgeable of the subtle nuances of how the mind operates on the surface and at deeper levels. The knowledge of those nuances took me a lifetime to examine and experience.

Once I came up with a systematic program to teach tennis players how to infuse silence in their mind while playing, it was not that much of a challenge to do it in other sports. The mind produces motion the same for a forehand-down-the-line winner as it does for a 300-yard drive. The difference in motion between golf and tennis is obvious. Tennis players, other than when they serve, are reacting to motion while golfers are initiating it. Nevertheless, motion originates in the mind identically in both sports. If you understand how to infuse silence in one, it is not that much of a stretch to teach someone how to infuse it in the other.

The program I developed, the Fluid Motion Factor, has had a profound effect on how sports are played and taught. I wrote this book to give athletes the intellectual understanding of how the program works and a few specific ways to access the Fluid Motion Factor. Remember those pictures that are really a picture within a picture? There is one that could either be a lampshade or the side portrait of a man, depending on which lines you put your attention on. In many ways, this is what this book and the Fluid Motion Factor program is all about—looking at the same situation you have always looked at, only from a unique and different perspective.

When I was a senior at Penn, I read Robert Pirsig's book, *Zen and the Art of Motorcycle Maintenance: An Inquiry into Values.* I was a great searcher in college—searching for life's meaning, for my purpose in life, and for what the world was all about. I was taken aback by Pirsig's book and I thought one day I would like to write a similar book—a book that would reveal how I understood life, without actually talking about life. That is what I have tried to do in this book. I doubt if I accomplished it as well as Pirsig; but it was a great joy making the journey.

This book is as much as an autobiography as it is a book about golf. It was written in a very short period of time, almost as if it was writing itself. It was an effortless project that felt like the culmination of a thirty-seven-year odyssey into sports and into life. I truly hope you enjoyed reading it. I would like to end by quoting one of my favorite passages from Pirsig's book:

"The truth knocks on the door and you say, 'Go away, I'm looking for the truth,' and so it goes away. Puzzling."

Testimonials

I have received over 100 testimonials on my program and I wanted to include some of them here. As you can see, golfers tend to pour out their heart and soul to me! The program is taught by me at David Leadbetter's international headquarters at ChampionsGate in Orlando and by Buddy Biancalana in Phoenix. I also teach an online coaches certification program that can be used for players wanting to improve their game. Our contact information is steven. yellin@davidleadbetter.com and bianc.buddy@gmail.com and our websites are fluidmotiongolf.com and zonetraining. net. We would love to teach you the program.

I had the great fortune to compete and win on the PGA

Tour. A few years ago I decided to stop playing and turn to teaching and coaching mostly because I am interested in talent and potential in others. To be the best coach I can be I have researched many disciplines. This is my short story of how the Fluid Motion Factor caught my attention.

Over the last 30 plus years Steven Yellin, founder of the Fluid Motion Factor, has been researching an athletic phenomenon that happened to him. Steven had this incredible zone experience in his first love, tennis. He knew there was a reason why, and he knew there was no reason why an athlete should not be able to reproduce the zone experience.

Shelly Liddick, the Women's Golf Coach at Bellevue University and the 2012 LPGA Coach of the Year, introduced me to Steven earlier this year in 2103. I used to work with Shelly's husband Chuck Hogan when I played my best golf and so when she said talk to Steven, I listened.

Steven and I met in San Antonio and he worked with me for three days teaching and explaining to me what he discovered. As he talked he described perfectly what happened to me when I won the 1996 Texas Open where I beat Tiger by one and Jay Haas by two. As Steven talked I became fascinated with his message and I knew almost immediately the Fluid Motion Factor program was more than a theory, but the reality of what happens when we play well.

In my professional career I would float in and out of this experience. To be honest, I thought the Zone experience was a matter of luck or chance. The more Steven talked, the more I became absolutely convinced that the Zone is not a matter of chance but can be produced at will. Thus my teaching has changed and this is my question to you. If I told you I can teach you how to get into the zone at will and command would you believe me?

Right now, right here you have the opportunity to learn how to put yourself into the Zone, quiet your mind, and access your very best golf swings more consistently. Since meeting Steven and practicing the Fluid Motion Factor with every shot I have played since April, my personal performance has been as good as it can get. I teach and thus I practice very little yet my scores remain par or better almost every time I play.

One of the byproducts of the Fluid Motion Factor Program is my conventional putting has come back to me. With January 1, 2016 looming to play professional golf you will need to putt conventionally. The Fluid Motion Factor Program has dramatically restored this part of my game. Imagine what you would do if you made more putts?

Furthermore I have seen a 100% increase in performance in every client I have seen and shared Steven's program. I have had almost a dozen clients shoot their lowest scores ever and one female won with maybe the worst swing ever but in the state of fluid motion. I bring that up because the evidence tells us that a perfect swing does not guaranty success. The mini-tours are full of talented players with great swings and loads of desire. The question is how do you get from the mini-tour to the PGA Tour? Steven's program has the answer.

I am convinced that the information Steven Yellin has, and the way he presents it will alter the way golf is taught in the future. What is going to separate you from the rest of the guys seeking to be on Tour? If I told you I can give a very legal and very unfair advantage over your competitors who almost all believe their success is wrapped up in their golf swings would you seize that advantage? I will tell it to you straight. If I was 25 and not 55 I would embrace what Steven has to offer and ride it to the Tour. What he has to tell you is exactly what I experienced every time I played well on Tour. We will teach you how to do this on purpose, at your will, whenever you want.

I tell my high school players all the time I would muse on Tour, "If I had known then what I know now I would have been so much better." Well if you want to know now what you will discover too late, now is the time. If you want to know what over thirty years of research as to how the mind and body work and almost thirty years of tournament golf knows, now is the time.

David Ogrin, PGA Tour Winner

Dear Steven,

I would like to thank you for bringing the true joy back in my game as well as for my son. It has been an amazing summer. I played college golf but suffered from a mental block that kept me from truly reaching my potential. I solved putting yips with a long putter 25 years ago but since then it hit my chipping so bad that I built a long chipper that I used for 3 years! I was introduced to your program at Rick McCord's academy and since then my handicap went from 6.5 to 1.8. My son also bought into your program and has gone from 10 handicap to 5! The best however was during a trip this summer to Scotland, when my son Brandon aced the Postage Stamp at Royal Troon!

Jeff Waaland

Steven,

I really think what you have done has never been done before. You have scratched an itch that I have had for 40 years of teaching and playing.

I have been on the Golf Magazine "Top 100 Teachers" list since its inception in 1992. I have talked to many teachers and psychologists over the years that have never been able to explain the elusive "aha" moments that you describe so well in your program.

I would like spend some time with you if possible. You can click on my website below if you need more information about me and my academy.

I really was excited and impressed with what you presented in your that I would love to see and learn more.

Thank you,

Rick McCord
Director of Instruction
The McCord Golf Academy at Orange Lake

Steven,

I have been playing golf for 45 years, 20 years as an amateur and 25 years as a Professional. I've been teaching the game for 25 years and during those 25 years have taken lessons from the best instructors in the world and also spent hours in seminars with the best sports psychologists in the States. I did this for my own game but mostly for my teaching. I always knew there was something that the best players were doing to be at that level and it was not technique alone. After the tapes and the book I know that you have something very special and seem to answer a lot questions on what are the better players really doing different than the average players. I can't wait to work more with you and Quiet Mind Golf for myself and my students.

Thanks,

PGA Professional, Jim Muschlitz

Steven,

The process we have been going through together, as you have been imparting your wisdom and pure genius concerning complete freedom in sports motion and activity, has been absolutely amazing! We have had maybe six or seven sessions and it has been a total transformation in my inner game from normal frustration mixed with moments of great enjoyment when I hit a great shot, sink a putt, or chip it in, every once in a while. Now I play with a feeling of great confidence, with much greater repetition of pure shots, and I never thought I would experience such joy in sport! I have not practiced a great deal this year and yet when we played two weeks ago I hit six fairways in a row with my tee shot. I felt maybe one mishit in nine holes with all my full swings. What really amazed me, though, was how easy it felt AND how enjoyable it was. While it was not the lowest score ever, it is easy to say it was the most enjoyable game of golf I have ever played! I feel confident that with just a little more work getting your wisdom incorporated into my short game I will be shooting amazingly low scores that I would never have dreamed possible!

It seems so little to say thank you for so profoundly changing what has been an important part of my life for over 50 years.

Great Success and Best Wishes Always,

Chris Wege

Steven,

Yesterday we played at the Sand Ridge club a little east of Cleveland. It's a very good Tom Fazio course that was ranked in Golf Digest's top 100. In any event, the 17th hole, par 3 was playing at 203 yards. I used a 3 hybrid that, before your program, I had NO CHANCE beyond a lucky roll to the green. Yesterday, I hit a high, tight draw that landed 8 yards short of the pin and rolled in for my 7th hole-in-one. I cannot tell the following to anyone else but you and Rick McCord: After setting my stance and looking at the pin, I visualized the surfboard back to the ball, buried anything past the ball on the tee, and I do not recall hitting the shot except looking up and watching the flight. Just like the old Timex watch, It's still working!!

I am heading back to Florida in early October and looking forward to more and better golf.

All the best, and thanks again for your inspiration,

Rick Assini

My name is JD Goodfellow. I am a sophomore at West High School in Iowa City, Iowa. I have played golf my whole life and I have played in many junior golf tournaments during the summer over the past couple of years. Also, I currently play 1 or 2 on my high school golf team.

I first met Steven Yellin on the range when he was giving a clinic on his Fluid Motion Golf program. After watching and listening to his clinic I knew he could help me improve my own golf game. Since the clinic I have met with him personally twice, read his book, and watched the videos. Steven's program has had a positive effect on all parts of my game. This program has helped me clear my mind on the golf course. Although I don't hit every shot perfect, my misses get me in less trouble. I am hitting more accurate solid shots on the course which is helping to lower my scores. I have also seen an increase in distance when I'm hitting the ball. Not only has his program helped me with the irons and my driver, it's also helped me with my chipping and putting. With the Fluid Motion Program I am chipping my shots a lot closer to the hole and I am making more putts from all distances. The program helps me clear my mind when I'm putting which is very important with the short knee knocker putts.

Using the Fluid Motion Program I have shot 3 of my lowest competitive rounds of golf in tournaments. Overall I am hitting the ball much more solid and further, my chips are closer to the hole and my putts per round have gone down.

A couple of months ago Steven introduced his program to our golf program at Clayton State University. I understood right away that what Steven had realized after thirty years of studying was revolutionary and something that I knew would help me to constantly perform on a higher level. After my first experience of how effortless a round of golf can be played with fluidity in the mind I was hooked. It was an in-the-zone experience where I felt like I could do anything with the ball. This is what will happen when the signals from the brain go straight to the motor system which activates the fast-twitch muscles. This program has helped me to take the next step in my career and I'm convinced that it can help everyone.

Fredrik Lindblom
Three college wins
Ping All American

I had attempted the PGA Player's Ability Test (PAT) multiple times and was unable to shoot the qualifying score. A week prior to my next scheduled PAT, I was introduced to the Quiet Mind process.

The PAT requires 36 holes of golf in one day. Within the first three holes, I found myself struggling mentally. I was able to implement the Quiet Mind process during that round which allowed me to continue to shoot well below the target score for the entire 36 holes. I shot a 73 to lead the field the first day and then cruised in with a 75. Most notably, my putting became more fluid and as the day progressed my confidence improved dramatically. I attribute my success to Quiet Mind.

Scott Riley
PGA Professional

Dear Steven,

I can't thank you enough for your program…it worked great. I am a single digit handicapper and yet have been struggling with the mental side of this game for over 25 years. I could never understand why I and almost every golfer I ever watched had such a smooth fluid practice swing and yet their swing with the ball was choppy and fast. Now I know why. I used to teach golf and limited how much technical instruction I would give because technically they were fine during their practice swing but their real swing was a mess. Would try to work on their thought process of relaxing and trying to stay calm to no avail. I got so frustrated with my own game and the lack of fluidity in my swing that I was about ready to look for a new sport after playing for 35 years until trying your program. After one day of practicing your drills I played a round with some of the best ball striking I've ever done. Had developed a nervous twitch where I would let go and re-grip my club during the swing but after your program that twitch was gone and truly felt like I was hitting my real shots like my practice swing, fluid and in balance. One thing that struck me about your program was your comment that thoughts cannot create fluidity in your swing, which is what I've been trying to do for 25 years. No matter how much I told myself to calm down it never worked. Your comment about time was true as well when I used to hit shots I felt like I blacked out and couldn't even remember the process of swinging it seemed to happen so fast, but yesterday on the course I could actually feel parts of my swing as time did seem to slow down. I read so many sports psychology books but none of them ever worked until your program, which is so simple it's hard to believe it works but boy does it. If you ever need video testimony of your program don't hesitate to contact me. I'd love to come down and meet you, your program is brilliant well done.

Regards,

Jim Johnson
Temecula, Ca

Steven,

I have been working with your program for a couple months and 2 weeks ago I shot the lowest round of my life (66). I am 5 handicap player and have only been under par a few times previously, but not close to 6-under round. My ball striking was far from perfect, but I seemed to be in such a zone on the greens, I was seeing and making everything. I love the program and am trying every shot and every round to find my zone. I keep trying because I want to shoot 65!

Mark

I don't want to bore you too much with my tale of golf, but I have to tell you how well the program is working. I have been a 12–14 handicap, but recently it has dropped to a 9. This past week has been incredible. Although I have broken 80 many times, it is always my goal in the back of my mind. On Tuesday I played with a high schooler from the longer tees and shot 35 on the front nine. The next day I opened with a double, then a bogey and stayed calm with 9 at 3 drill and shot 75. Yesterday I just couldn't score and was 9 over after the 12th hole. I kept my calm, continued the drills and went 1 under on the last six to shoot 79 (par at our course is 71). It is in great part due to your program, I stayed focused and calm and believe I am only going to play better. The area code drill for putting is incredible beyond belief. I am able to strike the putt so freely if I just think the last number as I strike the ball.

Thank you, thank you, thank you.

Richard

My name is Clark Nelson and I have read your book and have seen some of your online videos. I am on the Clayton State Golf team and I believe you have talked with my coach Steve Runge. I really enjoyed the book, as I have been struggling with too many swing thoughts and not trusting my own ability. However, I now have no swing thought at all, which I thought I could not do. I always felt like I had to have swing thoughts. I now can feel myself save shots far easier because I'm using fluid motion like you talk about in your book. Thanks for this. It was a great eye-opener.

Clark

Dear Steven,

I watched the video segments today before I went out to play this evening. While I've broken 80 once or twice before tonight, and usually play from a longer tee, I shot my first under par 9 on the front with a 34. Ended up two over at 74. Easily the lowest score I've shot to date. Very excited to continue to develop and understand these drills.

Michael F.

Steven,

As someone who has had sports as the center of his life, working with Steven and his golf mental program has been a life-changing experience. I played semipro hockey for 15 years in New England and have been a teaching tennis Pro for 20 years and an avid golfer for six years. I met him five years ago and he changed the paradigm of playing and teaching tennis, but recently I have worked with him in golf and tennis and I can't think of any knowledge in sports that could even approach this knowledge. I truly believe it will change sports forever, because if one doesn't start with the mind, they will always be forgetting the top priority and always be lacking in success. But a crucially important aspect is the dramatic increase in enjoyment, which is really what sports is all about and is what everyone is missing unless all the processes are reduced to effortlessness. The body and mind are happy when in a fluid and effortless state. It's only icing on the cake when it also produces much greater success.

Dave Townsend

Acknowledgments:

I first want to acknowledge and thank my partner, Buddy Biancalana. Buddy is a dear friend for life and together, we are doing something very special in the world of sports.

I want to thank my parents, Jerry and Helene, for the deep love and wisdom they have imparted to me that helped me grow as a person. They are the best parents in the world and I cannot thank them enough for all they have given me.

I want to thank David Leadbetter for his support of the Fluid Motion Factor program and for inviting me to teach the program at his fabulous world headquarters at Champions Gate in Orlando. David knew there was something missing in the game, and the Fluid Motion Factor program fills in that much-needed gap.

I also want to thank Rick McCord for his friendship and for his deep insights into the program that help take it to another level. Rick is a *Golf Magazine* Top 100 teacher and has a brilliant mind for the game. We have spent many an hour talking about the profound insights this program affords all golfers. Rick, I owe you many a dinner at Carrabba's and hopefully I will be able to take you there for many, many years.

In 1975 my mother called me and said she had just seen Maharishi Mahesh Yogi, the founder of the Transcendental Meditation program, on the Merv Griffin show, along with Clint Eastwood and Mary Tyler Moore. My mother is a spiritual person and said to me that if Merv Griffin can meditate, then she could also learn to meditate and wanted to know if I wanted to learn as well. We then both learned together. It changed my life. It allowed me to experience deep silence twice a day that was instrumental in understanding how dynamic motion emerges from a quiet mind. I doubt this program could ever have been developed without experiencing that rich silence on a daily basis.

Steven Yellin has a company that has worked with professional athletes in seven sports. These include players from the PGA, LPGA, MLB, NBA, NHL, NFL, and the PBA. He co-authored the book, The *7 Secrets of World Class Athletes* with Buddy Biancalana. He has also produced instructional videos in golf and bowling and has developed an online certification program for golf professionals. That program can also be used by every level of golfer to improve their game. He still competes in tennis tournaments around the country and is one of the top twenty players in the county in his age division. Though tennis is his first love, he still hits golf balls every day as he finds the sound and feeling of a well-hit golf ball to be a spiritual experience hard to put into words.